© 2013 Debbie Sessions
All rights reserved.

ISBN-10: 0988654105
ISBN-13: 978-0-9886541-0-5

For a digital PDF copy of this book please email a copy of your receipt to debbie@vintagedancer.com. Thank you for your purchase.

Table of Contents

Introduction   page 2
Women's FASHION HISTORY   page 4
Women's CLOTHING   page 7
The Victory Suit   page 7
Dresses   page 10
Blouses   page 15
Sweaters   page 17
Pants   page 18
Coats   page 19
Play Clothes   page 21
Swimwear   page 23
The Working Girl   page 25
Eveningwear   page 27
The Teenager   page 29
Wedding Dresses   page 30
The Rebel Girls   page 32
The New Look   page 32

Women's ACCESSORIES   page 33
Shoes   page 33
Vintage, Reproduction or New shoes?   page 36
Hats   page 36
Bags   page 38
Gloves   page 40
Jewelry   page 40

The UNDERWEAR   page 43
Lingerie   page 43
Modern Girdles - Advice for Creating the 1940's Shape   page 45
Hosiery   page 46
Sleepwear   page 47

The BEAUTY   page 48
Hair   page 49
Makeup   page 55

Men's FASHION HISTORY   page 58
Men's CLOTHING   page 59
Suits   page 59
Casual Trousers   page 61

Collared Shirts   page 62
Casual Shirts   page 63
Sweaters   page 64
The Zoot Suit   page 65
Formal Wear   page 66
Military and Work Wear   page 67
Swimwear   page 69
Sleapwear   page 69
Underwear   page 70
Outerwear   page 71

Men's ACCESSORIES   page 73
Hats   page 73
Shoes   page 75
Socks   page 77
Belts   page 78
Watches   page 78
Cufflinks   page 78
Pocket Squares   page 79
Scarfs   page 79
Ties   page 79
Hairstyles   page 80

Advice for Dressing as a 1940's Man   page 81
Men's Shopping   page 82

Making a 1940'S OUTFIT   page 83
Sewing with Vintage Patterns   page 83
Modifying Modern Patterns   page 84
Hire a Seamstress   page 85

SHOPPING   page 86
What to look for   page 86
Shopping Online   page 88

Show and Tell   page 88

Resources   page 90

Contact Me   page 91
About the Author   page 92

Introduction

Have you ever watched an old 1940s movie and fallen in love with the clothes, or been to a swing dance party and admired the dancers strutting their Zoot Suit fashion? Are you a theatrical costumer working on a 1940s era project or an author writing a book set in the 1940s?

If any of these or countless other situations have inspired you to dress in 1940s fashions then you are not alone. I too fell in love with 1940s fashion and immediately jumped on the web to find the clothes I wanted to wear. I was expecting to find what I needed quickly and easily but unfortunately, the information online is too vague, too hard to find, too focused on cheap Halloween costumes and the list goes on and on. When I looked at books on fashion I became even more frustrated. They were either so focused on the historical details that they forgot to talk about what makes the style stylish, or they were only focused on high fashion, rather than everyday clothes. Why was there not one good site or one good book that would tell me what to wear, how to wear it, and where to shop? Bingo! The idea for this book was born.

My name is Debbie Sessions (previously Debbie Wells,) and I am fascinated by many eras of clothing from the Regency period through the 1960s. I have made my own Halloween and theatrical costumes since I was four years old. I have always loved to go through my mom's closet of vintage clothing inherited from our family members. It wasn't until I discovered vintage dancing that I realized there was a community of people who love to get dressed up in old clothing styles like me and my husband. I started www.vintagedancer.com to help vintage clothing and costume enthusiasts find clothing and accessories online, whihc is often not an easy task. While I love building my website, shopping pages and blogging about history and clothing, writing a book has given me so many more opportunities to say everything that needs to be said in one place.

The purpose of this book is to provide three important things:

1. History.
I admit I am a history nut, and I want to know why clothes are the way they are. It is an important part in understanding what makes 1940s clothing so different from the eras before and after, but I will not overwhelm you with history. Each topic in this book includes only as much history as needed to define the style.

2. Advice.
Trying to dress in 1940s style with today's modern expectations can be a challenge. I will give you tips and advice along the way to help you style yourself with maximum comfort and minimal cost. If you are on a budget the tips here will help you get the 1940's look at a price tag you can afford.

3. Shopping.
What good is all this information without telling you where to shop? There are hundreds of web stores that have everything you need for a 1940s outfit, but finding these stores is like looking for a needle in a haystack. I've done the hard work for you and found the best of the best online, many of which never show up in Google searches

Copyright and Disclosure:
Hundreds of hours by many different people have gone into creating this book. If someone shared this book with you without paying for additional copies, first thank them. Obviously, they think this book is an excellent resource. Second, I want you to scold them for breaking copyright laws. Copying this book in whole or part without the author's permission is against the law. Just do not do it and everyone stays happy.

The photographs and drawings in this book come from a variety of sources. Each image is identified with the copyright owner and website. If no copyright information is listed, the image is in the Public Domain or is part of my personal collection.

The 1940s Style Guide. All Rights Reserved. Debbie Sessions.

Enough legal mumbo jumbo- let's get to the

Women's fashion history

1933 dress outfit
Dover Clip Art

The 1940s were defined by a clean and slim silhouette, with a slightly military feel. Jackets, blouses, sweaters and skirts were short and close-fitting, all unadorned, and with the requisite sharp shoulder pads. Long sleeves were out, dresses were casual, and pants and "playsuits" became everyday attire for women.

Before World War II, Paris was the epicenter of fashion. All of the new styles originated there, and anonymous American designers simply copied the looks from France for their wealthy clientele or for department stores. The 1930s are best remembered for glamour, despite the Great Depression. Hollywood starlets were clothed in long, draped and flowing gowns made of satin, crepe, silk and velvet. Dresses and gowns were often bias cut on the diagonal, so it would cling to curves. During the 1930s, Coco Chanel brought the day suit into fashion, pairing a fitted jacket with a long skirt. Fur, whether as a coat, stole or collar, was the most desirable luxury item of the 1930s.

After Germany invaded France, including Paris, in 1940, many French designers closed their fashion houses, some fleeing the country. Those that stayed could not export their clothing or designs. The rest of the world, including America, was left to fill the fashion vacancy and come up with new designs, independent of the French design houses. New York City took over as a new fashion capital, creating a look that was influenced by the war going on across the ocean in Europe.

Alot of the fabric and materials normally used for clothing, shoes and accessories became scarce during World War II. Wool was used to make uniforms and coats for the soldiers, and leather was needed for their boots. Silk, normally used to make dresses, undergarments and stockings, was turned into parachutes and waterproof maps. Metal and various chemicals were needed to make weapons and other wartime essentials.

A woman donating her silk stocking to the war effort

1940's Style Guide

Ladies waiting in line for rationing coupons

Simply dressed woman with her army soldier

1949 DuPont nylon ad

Civilian clothing had to resort to using new materials in place of those made unavailable by the needs of war. Nylon, created by DuPont in 1938, replaced silk for women's items early in the war, but later began to be used for the same purposes as silk by the military. American cotton began to take over as a casual fabric of choice, while wool blends were introduced to reduce the amount of wool in civilian clothing and allow more wool for military uses. The synthetic fabric, rayon, became the most widely used fabric of the time. A softer, silkier version was used for day dresses, and a thicker version replaced wool for suits and coats. A new synthetic, "Vinylite" could be used instead of leather, and different types of plastic were used for all kinds of fashion applications.

Aside from breakthroughs in man-made materials, fashions of the day were most affected by the government clothing restrictions in place for the duration of the war. The very silhouette that dominated the '40s was the result of war. In Britain and elsewhere in Europe, ration coupons for clothing were given out on top of the manufacturing restrictions, and these often did not go far. The United States avoided rationing or coupons by putting strict rules in place for manufacturers. The only clothing items that were rationed in the U.S. were leather shoes, starting in 1943. These were only available in black, white, navy blue and brown.

The United States Production Board put into place "Limitation Orders" or Order L-85 governing women's clothing, which remained in effect until 1946. These restrictions were much less severe than those in Europe, but still greatly limited the style and appearance of women's fashions. The length and width of blouses, skirts and dresses was restricted by Order L-85, as was sleeve length and hip width. The number of pockets, buttons, pleats and seams was dictated, and most decorations were not allowed. This came to be known as the 'no fabric on fabric' rule. The colors of fabrics were set each season to conserve chemicals, so only a handful of patriotically named hues were available. The heels on shoes could only be 1 ½ inches high.

All of this interference resulted in a slim, uncluttered look. Skirts were shorter and tighter than anyone had seen before, and shirts and jackets were plain and practical. As the prices of clothes soared due to the shortages, garments had to last longer and go further. Pieces were extremely well-tailored and the styles were worn for a multitude of occasions. Although evening-wear was still produced and worn, people began to dress more casually on many occasions, including in restaurants and theaters. Versatile separates and sportswear took over in place of special dress for different occasions, and women began to wear pants as a safety precaution while working in factories throughout the United States.

1940's Style Guide

1947 New Look
Dover Clip Art

Home sewing became more popular during the war years. In Europe, fabric could be had for fewer coupons than a ready-made garment. In the United States, pattern sales skyrocketed. Citizens were encouraged to mend old clothes, recycle old fabrics into new garments and combine dresses to make new ones. Pamphlets with titles like "Make Do and Mend," and "Make It Do Until Victory" showed women how to fix and care for their clothes to make them last, and how to make clothing from other household items like blankets and curtains, as well as how to remake adult garments into clothing for growing children.

The plain and functional styles dictated by wartime restrictions lasted throughout World War II. When U.S. restrictions were lifted in 1945 and 1946, women continued to wear their wartime garb. Softer and brighter colors returned to women's wardrobes and skirts got a little bit longer and flouncy.

In 1947, up-and-coming Paris designer, Christian Dior, showed his debut collection, soon to be dubbed the "New Look." The "New Look" was the total opposite of the uncluttered, straight and severe styles of the war years. The silhouette was much softer, creating an extreme hourglass figure, with the assistance of a corset and bust and hip padding, and the skirts were enormous confections of fabric.

The "New Look" didn't immediately take off in the United States. Women felt that Parisian designers had acted as though no war had taken place while they sacrificed for the war effort. However, most were also ready for a change, and as soldiers came back from the war, women stopped working and returned to new homes and cars in the suburbs. The economy prospered, and clothing manufacture became cheaper and easier, thanks to new methods devised during the war. New York and California remained in the fashion game, and American designers started to be known by name. While it took a few years, eventually women adopted Dior's "New Look" and it became the style of the 1950s.

1940's Style Guide

Women's clothing

The victory suit

The most iconic look of the war years was the two-piece suit. In the United States, it was patriotically called the victory suit, and, in Britain, it was the utility suit. The suit was practical and versatile, worn very often. The jacket and skirt could be mixed with other pieces, and a different blouse underneath could change up the look. The style did not change throughout the war, so that women wouldn't have to buy new clothes. The suit was popular for both day-wear and office work-wear, and could be dressed up with hats and jewelry for dinner or the theater. The look itself was carried over from the women's suits that appeared in the 1930s, but with significant differences to accommodate clothing restrictions.

The most commonly used fabrics for suits were wool-weight rayons, wool blends and lightweight wools. Limitation order L-85 said that the fabric for skirts must be non-wool or wool of 9-ounce weight or less. There was a limited color range to choose from because of dye restrictions, and most suits were in practical colors like black, grey, navy blue, green, brown and red. Plaids and checks were popular, as were pinstripes on black, navy or grey. Suits were tailored to fit and made to last. They were popular throughout the decade, with styles changing very little, even after the war, until 1948 and 1949, when skirts became longer and fuller.

Mid 1940's Suit
Hollyvoguevintage.com

1940's Kolmer suit
Pastperfectvintage.com

1940's Style Guide

For jackets, the sleeve length was restricted to 30 inches, and only single collars were allowed. Jackets had to be single-breasted, and were generally short, falling to between the low waist and just above the hip. They could have anywhere from one to seven buttons, with three to five favored. The sleeves could be full-length or short, but a three-quarter length was preferred for its versatility. Collars were pointed, and were usually small with thin lapels. Many jackets had no pockets at all, while others had two, one on each side. Fabric for patch-style pockets was restricted, so patch pockets were small or were replaced by inside slit pockets. The jacket was fitted, and somewhat narrower at the waist. It was often unlined, although it did not have to be. No jacket would be complete in the '40s without shoulder pads. These stuck out sharply, with square ends, giving a military feel to the overall look. Jackets were worn buttoned up all the way, with either a collared blouse or nothing at all underneath. Another popular style for the matching

Two sisters in mid to late 40s skirts, blouses and suit jackets

Late 1940's suit
Pastperfectvintage.com

suit jacket was the bolero, made from the same material as the skirt, just like the more common button-front style. The shape of the bolero was somewhat different. It was waist-length or even a little shorter, and could be long or short-sleeved. The front opening had rounded edges without a fastener or closed with one to two buttons. Many times there was no collar on the bolero, but some had a rounded collar, extending into thin, rounded lapels. A blouse was always worn under the bolero.

A third jacket style was the peplum jacket, again made to match the skirt. Peplum jackets were fitted in the bodice and flared from the waist. These jackets were wider at hemline than the waist, emphasizing a narrow waistline. The peplum could be anywhere from a few inches long to hip-length. Peplum jackets had long sleeves and buttoned down the front, and were worn with blouses underneath.

1947 grey suit with matching jacket

Bolero jacket
Vintagetrends.com

1940's Style Guide

Skirts were more restricted by Order L-85 than jackets. They could have no more than a 78 inch sweep, but were often much narrower. Skirts could not be lined, could not have belts or belt loops, and could not have a large number of pleats, tucks, shirring or gathers at the waist. This made for a straight, fitted skirt, but not tight by today's standards. The World War II-era skirts were more of an A-line shape, rather than a pencil skirt. In the United States, skirts often had one or two pleats in the front and a kick-pleat in the back to allow for easier movement. For the first time, short was in! Skirts typically sat at the waistline, without pockets, and fell to just below the knee, fastening on the side with a metal zipper and button at the top. As metal grew scarce during the war, buttons were used in place of zippers. The skirt almost always matched the color of the jacket, but was also worn separately with blouses or sweaters, or a combination of a plaid jacket with a plain skirt might be worn.

1946 suit dress with dolman sleeves and a pencil skirt, a look that carried into the 1950s

A-line skirt
Simplicityisbliss (etsy.com)

Late 40s Skirts; fuller, with pleats and pockets, than skirts of the early 40s

 1940's Style Guide

Dresses

Along with the Victory Suit, dresses were worn for both home and day-wear, but could also be dressed up for evening wear. Dresses of the 1940s stuck to a basic shape, although the bodices took several different forms. Order L-85 allowed for no more than 56 inches of fabric at the hip, and 78 inches for the sweep. Pleats, tucks and shirring were allowed above the waistline, but were restricted to using only 10 percent of the material, with a maximum of two pockets allowed.

Dresses were made from rayon, sometimes thicker and wool-like, but most often rayon crepe or flowing rayon jersey. Cotton was also used for summer dresses. Dresses were much more colorful than suits. They could be plain, in blues, greens and reds, but patterns in a rainbow of colors were frequently used for dresses. Small floral patterns in blues, purples, pinks and yellows were popular, as well as gingham checks and colorful stripes. A wartime pattern, using patriotic red, white and blue colors and a 'V' for victory motif was common. After the war, Hawaiian prints became very popular for women's dresses. Decorations like bows, ruffles and lace were rare, and most dresses were made of just one fabric and undecorated. For fancier styles, sometimes a bow was used to tie the collar or the collar was made of lace. Home seamstresses might repurpose other garments or linens to decorate their basic dresses.

There were a few different options for the bodice of the dress, but all of them used the sharp, square 1940s style shoulder pads. Dress shoulder pads were a little bit less pronounced than those for the suit jacket. The top fit much like a blouse, fitted but not tight, and especially snug at the waist.

The sleeves could be full-length or three-quarter length, but were usually short, hitting from two inches above the elbow to elbow length. Sleeves weren't tight and were often gathered or puffed at the shoulder, allowing space to move and work in the dress. If the sleeves were long, they were typically full, but tight at the wrist with a buttoned cuff.

Two shirtdress styles

Shirtwaist dress
Retrowardrobe.com

1940's Style Guide

The most popular dress style was the shirtwaist. The top of the dress looked like a button-down blouse, with a small, pointed shirt collar or a small, rounded peter pan collar. A row of buttons fastened the front of the dress; usually four to six medium sized ones that went down to the waistline, but some shirtwaist dresses had buttons all the way down the front of the dress. Shirtwaist dresses sometimes had one or two pockets on the front, and were a practical, attractive and wearable choice for women at home, in the office or around town.

Cross-front dresses were another popular choice during the war years. Fabric draped from one side to the other, forming a V-neck with no collar, much like today's wrap dresses, but only through the bodice. However, unlike dresses of today, the neckline was not low and did not expose the chest or cleavage. The draped fabric attached at the opposite side, either at the waistline or more often several inches above the waistline, creating a slight empire line and a more modest V-neck.

Shirring was also used to create a feminine dress bodice while accommodating the fabric restrictions of the war. The neckline was a narrow V shape. Like the cross-front dress, this was not low-cut and had no collar. Shirring, or threads that pulled the fabric into rows of gathers, was used either at the bust, with two shirred panels defining the bustline of the dress, or at the waist, with shirred panels at either side. The rest of the top was constructed of plain, flat fabric. Dresses shirred at the bust had an empire-waist style top, with shirring through the bust and a flat panel of fabric fitted around the torso from under the shirred bust to the waistline.

The two most common 1940s women's looks- a suit and a collared dress. Cross front dress on the left and shirtwaist dress on the right.

Reproduction tea length shirtwaist dress
Vivienofholloway.com

1940's Style Guide

The skirts of all 1940s dresses were basically A-line, but it was often gathered slightly and was always slightly fuller than the suit skirt, starting from the waistline. Dresses were also made from softer fabrics, so the skirts flowed and had some swing to them. Shirtwaist dresses usually had skirts that used less fabric than the other two styles, but they were all far from fluffy or full. Like suits, dresses were relatively short, coming to just below the knee. There could be two pockets on either side of the skirt for more casual styles or those intended for wear at home, but this wasn't a necessity.

While shirtwaist dresses buttoned up the front, the other two styles were fastened at the back or side with a metal zipper, or small buttons once metal became scarce. With the possible exception of the shirred styles, dresses were always worn with a very thin, one-inch-thick or less, belt at the waist. The belt was most often a self-belt, made from the same fabric as the dress, but it could, less commonly, also be a thin leather or vinyl version. In the late 40s belts could be very wide.

Not all dresses followed the three bodice styles discussed above, but the skirts were similar for all dresses during the period. They were all made in the same materials and colors. Bodices were always fitted, but some were not a shirtwaist, cross-front or shirred. Some were just plain, but these had many different types of necklines. The necklines in the '40s were very high-cut compared to those of today, and would not show any cleavage. The square neckline was square shaped, usually a little bit wider at the bottom than the neck. The sweetheart neckline was about the same width and came to a point, with either side of the point rounding up and then curving out and around the neck. Imagine a heart shape on the front of the dress – the bottom of the neckline is shaped like the pointed end of a heart, with the empty space the heart would leave above it. The keyhole neckline was fitted around the neck, and a small, usually triangle-shaped piece, was cut out of the fabric at the neckline, with the point facing the top. A thin piece of fabric was left at the neck, or a fabric string tied into a small bow at the neck. The slit neckline looked like a very, very thin 'V,' only an inch or two wide at the top opening. All of these dress styles buttoned up the side or back, and some had metal zippers.

1940s swing dresses featured fuller skirts, often with pleats, puffed sleeves, and conservative necklines; most popular with teens and young women

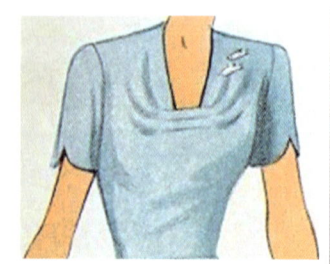

Square

Keyhole

Sweetheart

Slit

www.sovintagepatterns.com

1940's Style Guide 13

The "Kitty Foyle" dress was another popular daytime style, named after the movie of the same name starring Ginger Rogers. Rogers played a working girl earning a living in an office. The dress she sported in the movie, dark with a contrasting white collar, gave rise to this popular dress style and to the name 'white-collar girl,' referring to women office workers. The "Kitty Foyle" dress was often long-sleeved and shaped like other dresses of the period, with a fitted bodice and an A-line shaped skirt that came to just below the knees. It fastened with buttons either down the back or front, and was made of rayon or a wool blend. The dress was dark in color, often black, navy or red. A crisp, white pointed shirt collar, and sometimes cuffs as well, were the characteristic features of the "Kitty Foyle" dress. The collar could also be a rounded peter pan style, rather than a pointed shirt collar.

The peplum dress was popular for both daytime and slightly fancier occasions, depending on the look of the individual dress. It was made from rayon, and available in a variety of colors. Floral and other patterns were popular for peplum dresses. The bodice was fitted like other dresses of the '40s with shoulder pads and a straight or A-line skirt. The dress buttoned up the back or side. The distinguishing feature of this look was the peplum coming out from the waistline. This was a piece of the same fabric gathered and attached to the waistline at the top, falling anywhere from about six inches long to hip length. The peplum flared out from the waist, and sometimes a self-fabric belt was worn at the waistline at the start of the peplum.

Kitty Foyle dress

1947 shirred dresses

Chiffon dress
Pastperfectvintage.com

Peplum dress pattern
Sovintagepatterns.com

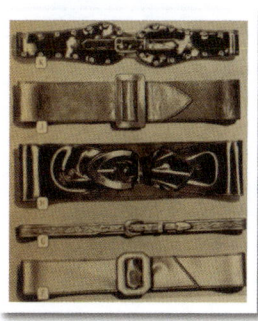

1947 belts both traditional thin and new wide belts

14 1940's Style Guide

For a more playful look, a fun summertime style was the apron dress, and it looked exactly like a dress with a coordinating apron. The apron dress was made out of cotton, and could be plain, but was more often a colorful pattern, like checks, plaids or florals. The dress was shaped like all of the other dresses, with a fitted bodice and gathered skirt. The apron dress fell from the waist to just below the knees, and buttoned down the back. These dresses were either short-sleeved or sleeveless, and had a rectangular panel of fabric down the length of the front of the dress with ruffled trim on both sides, matching the dress fabric. A fabric tie was attached to either side of this panel at the waist, and was tied in a bow at the back of the dress, forming the 'apron.' The neckline was usually square, and two large patch pockets were often sewn to the front of the dress. A variation was the pinafore dress, which was sleeveless and worn over a blouse.

Apron dress
Simplicityisbliss (Esty.com)

1947 pastel day dresses

Patriotic wrap dress
Timelessvixen.com

Colorful dress fabrics

1940's Style Guide

Blouses

Blouse styles have not changed dramatically in the past few decades, but every era has small distinguishing characteristics that differentiate its blouses. In the 1940s, Order L-85 placed some restrictions on women's blouses. There could only be one pocket, and if tucks or pleats were used a ruffle could not be, and vice versa. There could only be one ruffle per sleeve, only two bows per shirt and cuffs could not be more than three-inches wide. Blouses followed the same basic '40s trend of simplicity.

Blouses were made with rayon for a silkier look and with cotton for casual and work wear. Blouses were fairly short, between 20 and 25 inches usually, and sleeves were long and full, coming to a tight wrist-cuff, or short-sleeved hitting above the elbow. Shoulders were squared, and often puffed to create a softer and looser sleeve. Blouses were usually a plain color, like white, cream or black. Small plaids, checks and colorful stripes were also common. Blouses were worn tucked into skirts or pants, but were also worn underneath suit jackets.

1940's blouses
Sensibility.com

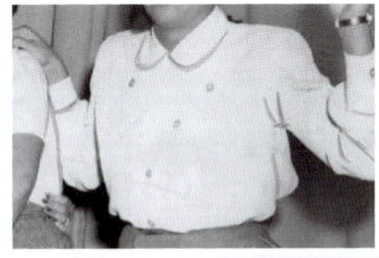

Long sleeve blouse

Striped short sleeve blouse

Jo Stafford wearing a short sleeve blouse

Blouses buttoned down the front and were usually worn buttoned up all the way. The collar was either a pointed shirt collar or sometimes a small, rounded peter pan collar. Most blouses were simple and plain, often without much decoration. Quite often, rayon blouses were tied at the neck with a large bow, and some had ruffles at the wrists or collar. Others had ruffles or lace trim down the center of the blouse. Blouses also sometimes had a tucks or pleats at the front of the shoulder. Collars and sleeves occasionally had lace trim, particularly if it could be reused from another garment.

Another trend in tops in the '40s was the more casual peasant-style blouse, made popular by Latin Hollywood film star Carmen Miranda. It was made of white cotton, and had short, puffed sleeves. It was loose-fitting with a scooped or square neckline, sometimes decorated with eyelet at the neckline and sleeves. The peasant blouse was worn with a gathered 'dirndl skirt,' made of colorful floral patterned or striped cotton, sitting at the waistline and flowing to a wide hem.

Peasant blouse
Mystiquevintage.com

Peasant blouse and dirndl skirt

Peasant skirts and blouses

Sweaters

Knitted sweaters were a clothing staple throughout the '40s. And like blouses, sweater styles haven't changed significantly through the years. Sweaters of the 1940s were made from cotton and wool-blends, or less often of wool yarn. They could be store-bought, but often women knitted their own, and hand-knit sweaters were a big part of the homemade clothing during the decade. Usually quite plain, sweaters were available in a wide variety of colors, including pastel and bright shades. Some of them had decorative embroidery on the fronts.

Sweaters usually had a high, rounded crew neck and were slightly fitted. They were fairly short, hitting above the hip. Several styles were especially popular; the long-sleeved crew-neck, the short-sleeved crew-neck, and the twin-set, which consisted of a crew-neck sleeveless sweater with a matching cardigan. Cardigans were sometimes a little bit longer than pullover sweaters, and were often decorated with a matching ribbon down the front button band. Sweaters were worn with both skirts and pants for a common day-wear look.

1947 striped knit top

Formal knit sweater
Vintagepatternplace (esty.com)

Hand knit sweater made by
www.facebook.com/pages/1940s-Style-For-You/

1940's Style Guide

Pants

Today, women wear pants every day, and have a pair for almost any occasion, but before the 1940s, women simply did not wear pants. As women began working in factories, while men were away at war, they started to wear pants out of necessity. Pants were much easier to work in than a skirt or dress, particularly in manufacturing jobs, where skirts could get caught in machinery and sitting in them proved to be less than modest. At first, pants were only worn while working, but as the '40s wore on women began to wear pants as everyday attire for home and day-wear for the first time.

The women's pants of the '40s were not exactly figure-flattering. The design was basically the same as men's pants, tailored, but not meant for the female form. Pants sat at the natural waistline, well above the belly button, much higher than today. They were tight around the waist, with a two-inch wide waistband. From there they had straight, wide legs that did not fit closely to the body. Imagine them making a triangle shape from top to bottom when laid flat.

Depending upon the style, pants had belt loops and were worn with a narrow leather or vinyl belt or were made without loops. Women's pants usually had two pockets on the sides and none on the back, since only two pockets were allowed by Order L-85 regulations. Slit pockets often came to mid-thigh. Pants were usually flat-fronted, but after the war, some styles were pleated.

They were hemmed at the bottom with no cuffs. In length, they came to a few inches from the ground, a bit short by modern standards. They, like women's skirts, were fastened on the side with buttons or a hidden metal zipper.

Pants were made from a variety of materials including wool-like rayon, cotton denim, cotton twill, cotton seersucker, wool flannel and wool blends. A lot of them were plain and practical in color, in shades including black, grey, navy or dark brown. Others came in stripes and checks. Pants were worn with flat shoes and a tucked-in blouse or sweater for casual, everyday occasions.

1940's reproduction trousers
Vivianholloway.com

Coats

Coats were restricted by L-85, but there were relatively few rules. Coats couldn't have a bi-swing back, could have no more than two pockets, and had a limitation on sleeve circumference, eliminating exaggerated sleeve styles. Most coats were made from wool and rayon-wool blends, often using re-purposed wool since wool fabric was needed for the war. Linings were made of rayon crepe or satin. Most coats followed the same basic style with a few variations. They came to a little bit below the knee, and were made in herringbone, tan, grey, dark green, navy and red, as well as other dark, practical colors. They were plain, without decoration, and all had large square shoulder pads.

One popular style during the 1940s was the wool trench coat. It was somewhat loose-fitting, but not baggy, with a pointed collar and one or two rows of buttons down the front. A belt about two inches thick tied or buckled at the waist. The trench usually had two slit pockets on the sides.

Another style of coat was slightly more fitted through the waist, flaring out slightly from there. It usually had one row of buttons, but could have two. It could have slit pockets on the sides or two large patch pockets on the front. The collar was pointed, but this type of coat also sometimes had a fur collar, typically fox fur. The fur collar would look like a small shawl draped over the top of the coat. Fur-trimmed coats were dressier and often had cloth-covered buttons or a cloth belt.

Wool box coat with white embroidery trim

1947 blue wool trench coat

Long coat
Simplicitybliss (etsy.com)

Faux fur box coat
Hollyvoguevintage.com

1940's Style Guide

One of the most popular styles was the polo or box coat. It was cut very straight and wide, in the shape of a box, and was oversized. These coats usually had two rows of buttons, but were also made with one row. Patch pockets embellished the front of the box coat.

Fur coats were worn, but mostly before and after the war, rather than during the war years. Fox and lamb were popular choices, and many cheaper furs were dyed to look like fox. Fur coats were cut straight and boxy, and were, like polo or box coats, fairly wide. Before the war, they were short, falling just below the waist. After, they were worn longer, reaching the knee.

1940s white rabbit fur cape

Peak lapel coat

1948 mink cape coats

Double breasted military style coat

Fur collar wrap often worn over coats and winter dresses

1940's Style Guide 21

Play Clothes

Play clothes sound like something little kids wear so they won't get dirty, but grown women during the 1940s wore what were called playsuits. These casual outfits were worn outdoors, either at the beach, in the backyard to catch some sun, or for sportswear. Playsuits were usually made of cotton, although they could also be found in rayon. They were brightly colored, in reds, greens, yellows and blues, and were often made in patterns, like checks and plaids, as well as floral and Hawaiian prints. The playsuit usually consisted of two to three pieces and there were several different styles.

The one-piece romper was a popular playsuit style. The top resembled a button-down blouse that came in at the waist and extended into shorts. A waistband defined the waist and separated top from bottom. The shorts fit much like the pants of the day – tight at the waist, loose and wide-legged, reaching to about mid-thigh. Buttons extended down the front of the shorts. A matching overskirt completed the outfit, creating the appearance of a dress. Button-down skirts were the most common choice, and the skirt was usually longer than the shorts, between low thigh and above knee length. This allowed modest women to wear the outfit anywhere and take off the skirt when appropriate.

Pant playsuit and two-piece with wrap over skirt

Playsuit
Swannegrace (esty.com)

Playsuit or Swimsuit
Pastperfectvintage.com

1940's Style Guide

Another popular type of playsuit had three pieces. It looked much like the one-piece, except the top was separate from the shorts and came with a shirtdress to cover both. Made in matching fabric, the separate top and shorts revealed a small amount of midriff. The '40s were the first time that this much skin was shown! It wasn't a lot, as the shorts fit at the natural waistline, just like all other bottoms worn during the period. The top ended only inches above the waistband. The tops were plain, buttoning up the back, and were often scoop-necked with short sleeves, but could also be halter tops. The halter straps were thick and either tied around the neck or crossed in the back. The halter was the same length as a regular top and fastened with buttons in the back. Like the one-piece romper, these outfits also had a matching skirt that buttoned or tied at the waistband of the shorts, creating the look of a two-piece outfit.

http://www.wearinghistorypatterns.com/products/1940s-Sailor-Girl-Playsuit-Pattern.html
– Pattern for a Sailor themed 1940s playsuit

http://www.vintagesuitsbymary.com
– Swimsuits and playsuits made to order

Floral pant play suit
Pastperfectvintage.com

Casual summer shoes perfect to wear with playsuits

Playsuit pattern
Sovintagepatterns.com

Fun sailing shorts
Retrowardrobe.com

Swimwear

Swimwear in the 1940s, like many other clothing items, was also becoming less modest. The midriff came into fashion in the '40s, in both playsuits and swimsuits. Swimsuits were tight, unlike the suits of previous eras. One-piece swimsuits were still popular, but the new two-piece suit had plenty of fans. The materials used to make modern swimsuits had not yet been invented, so suits were made from rayon jersey and rayon jersey blends with knit cotton linings. Swimwear featured stretchy control panels in the stomach, made from a new type of material called lastex, and bra cups in the bust to keep the figure looking good in the revealing, by '40s standards, suits. Suits were made in all colors, but patriotic colors were especially popular. Floral patterns and polka dots were also used. Since the fabric did not stretch, suits fastened with small metal zippers in the back.

The one-piece swimsuit of the 1940s looked like a very tight, short dress. Cleavage still wasn't shown in swimwear, so the V top was high enough to cover the bust, with thin shoulder straps and a bra top that resembled a full-coverage bra. The suit extended down into a tight skirt-style bottom that covered the backside completely. The back of the suit was even with the chest. The one-piece offered plenty of shaping, and sometimes had boning in the stomach area to offer additional support. A halter top was also popular, with straps that tied at the neck. A new feature of some one-piece suits revealed a little bit of skin, when a small triangle of fabric was cut out underneath the bust to show some stomach.

1947 one and two piece swimsuits

1940's Style Guide

The bikini was officially invented in 1946, and named after the Bikini Atoll in the South Pacific, where the U.S. performed nuclear tests. This suit was tiny, and although it came up higher, it more closely resembled the two-pieces we wear today. However, this wasn't the style of two-piece that was usually worn in the '40s. It was simply too revealing. Even before the bikini, women started wearing two-piece swimsuits that looked just like one-pieces cut in half. The top was a full-coverage bra top, either with two thin straps or a halter top. The bottom looked like a tight mini-skirt, starting from the waistline and covering the entire backside, or flaring from the waist into a short, fuller skirt. The bandeau top with strings attached to the center front tying at the neck also became popular with two-piece suits.

http://www.glamoursurf.com – Vintage swimsuits, playclothes, and lingerie.

Bikini Swimsuit

Reproduction swimsuit
Popinaswimwear.com

Tip:

It's very hard to find vintage swimwear. Vintage swimsuits are also uncomfortable, unlike modern swimsuit fit and fabrics. Thankfully, most reproduction swimsuits are made of modern Lycra material and refitted with modern construction techniques. Here are a few choice reproduction swimsuit makers:

http://www.popinaswimwear.com
– Retro style suits made in the USA
http://www.dillingerpinup.com
– A few very cute '40s and '50s swimsuits
http://www.mybabyjo.com/swimwear.htm
– Mostly '50s with some that double for '40s
http://www.vintagesuitsbymary.com
– Swimsuits and playsuits made to order
http://www.vintagedancer.com/swimsuits/
– New swimsuits with 40s and 50s style

1940's Style Guide

The Working Girl

The 1940s weren't all about play. Many of the men in the U.S. were drafted for the war. While they were off at training or fighting overseas, women were encouraged to leave their homes and work in all sorts of jobs, from office work to factories, most notably in munitions factories contributing to the war effort. Women were also recruited for direct service in the war, in both non-combat positions and as nurses.

In an office setting, women wore their normal clothes, like suits or rayon dresses. However, skirts were not practical for the factory and industrial work that women began to do during the war, and they had to dress differently. They wore either denim or cotton twill pants with a tucked in, short-sleeved button down blouse. Often, especially for munitions work, they wore the now-famous 'Rosie the Riveter' coveralls.

These were usually made of blue denim or heavyweight cotton canvas in brown, tan or blue, and buttoned down the front middle. They were loose-fitting throughout, although some were fitted in the waist to reduce bagginess and provide for a more flattering fit. They were often long-sleeved to offer protection, but could have short shirt-sleeves. Long-sleeved coveralls fit tightly around the wrists and ankles to avoid loose ends getting caught in machines. Most coveralls had breast pockets to keep pens and small tools in, and were often worn with a cotton blouse underneath. Factory workers had to tie up their hair so that it wouldn't get caught in machinery, using a turban, scarf or bandana.

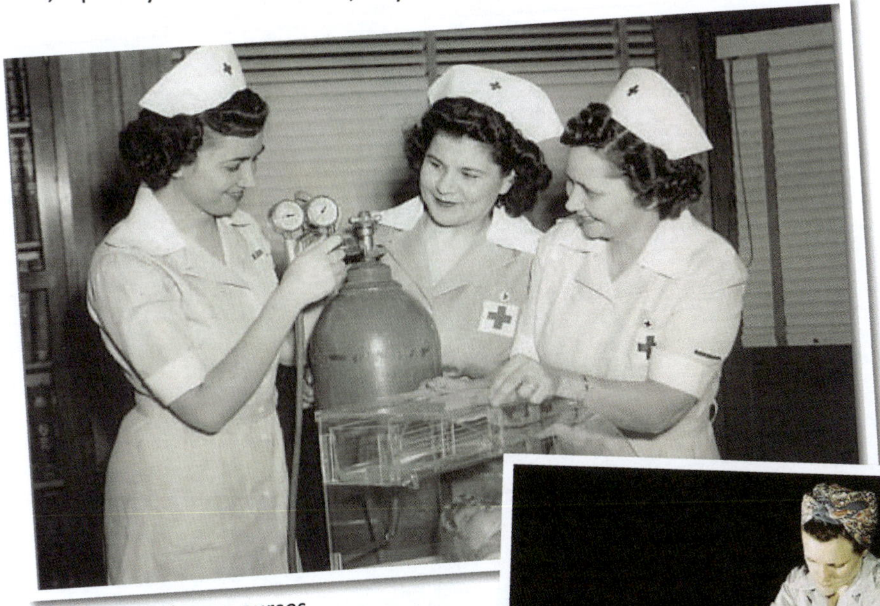

Red cross nurses

1940's Style Guide

Women didn't fight in the war, but they did join both the U.S. Army and U.S. Navy as clerical workers. Uniforms were stylish in an attempt to attract women to serve, and they looked much like suits that women were already wearing. The WAVES, Women Accepted for Voluntary Emergency Service, were part of the navy, and their uniforms consisted of a white blouse worn with a small navy scarf, underneath a navy jacket. The jacket was shaped like a suit jacket of the time, but slightly looser-fitting and with more severe shoulder pads. It had gold buttons down the front, with two breast pockets with matching gold buttons. The jacket sometimes had two gold, silver or bronze embroidered stripes and a star at the wrists, depending on the rank of the woman wearing it. This topped off an A-line navy skirt that came to the knee. A navy cap with a small brim, or sometimes a white cap with navy brim, was also worn. The WAC, Women's Army Corps, wore a very similar uniform. Instead of white and navy, the WAC uniform was all tan-colored, including the blouse. A tan tie went with the blouse, and a tan cap with a small brim was worn. The jacket had gold buttons as well.

Women also volunteered as nurses with the Red Cross during the war, many of them serving overseas. The uniform for nurses was a standard shape, but came in several colors, depending on the duties the nurse performed. It was a basic shirtwaist dress with a pointed collar and buttons all the way down the front, with a fitted bodice and A-line skirt. Nurses' dresses were a little bit longer than a regular skirt, reaching a couple of inches below the knee to allow them to bend and move modestly. They came in both short-sleeves and long, with the long sleeves coming to a cuff at the wrist. Made of cotton, they had a self-fabric belt at the waist. They were either grey or medium to light blue with a white collar and cuffs or white with white buttons and cuffs. The dresses had an embroidered Red Cross symbol on the left side of the chest, and were worn with a small, round white cap with a Red Cross symbol on the front. A shorter white cotton apron that tied in the back was worn over the dress when working. The front of the apron was square at the neckline and it had a large Red Cross symbol in the center.

1941 WAC uniform
Dover Clip Art

Navy women uniforms

Eveningwear

Eveningwear was the one area of fashion that still had glamour in the '40s. Sequins and beads were not rationed or restricted, and were put on everything. Dresses and gowns were simple but shiny, and were more casual than anything in the decades before or after the 1940s. Dresses were usually made from rayon jersey, taffeta or crepe and fastened with metal zippers or small buttons in the back. Black was the most popular color, but pinks, reds and blues were often used. Gowns were often covered head to toe in beads or sequins, with some decorated at the bust like a necklace, or down either side of the front, like a jacket lapel.

Satin evening dress
Timelessvixen.com

1946 evening suit
Dover Clip Art

Long black evening dress
Hollyvoguevintage.com

1940's Style Guide

One popular and stylish evening look during the '40s was the long gown and dinner jacket. The gown was columnar, long to the floor and straight. It was usually plain or had beading or sequins at the neckline. A dinner jacket, fitted and usually short to the waist, was worn on top of the dress. The dinner jacket was decorated with sequins and beads, either all over, or down the front, with square shoulder pads. It closed with buttons, often lavishly decorated with beading, or a metal zipper. A bolero jacket was also worn as a dinner jacket. These were short, coming to the waist, with rounded edges at the front. They had similar decorations and closed with a button at the top or middle or were worn open over the dress.

Other evening dresses were less fitted than the column gown, with long skirts that were a bit gathered, making them more flowing. Evening dresses were also worn shorter, just below the knee, with a similar flowing skirt. Skirts were sometimes draped to add movement. While evening dresses and gowns could have thin straps, they often had short or three-quarter length sleeves. If the dress had sleeves, it most likely had the ever-present sharp '40s shoulder pads. Fitted evening gowns often had shirring in the waist, with one panel on either side, or in the bust, or had a cross-front bodice. Evening dresses were usually high-cut in the neck, similar to day dresses of the time. They often had sequins, beading or other unrestricted decoration on some part or all of the dress or gown.

http://www.amazon.com/Vintage-Knitting-PATTERN-make-instructions/dp/B004CZOSV6
-Vintage knitting pattern to make a 1940s lace evening gown
http://www.etsy.com/shop/vintageousboutique
-Has a very nice selection of vintage formal gowns.
http://www.vintagedancer.com/1940s/1940-prom-dresses
-New 40s style formal dresses

Young woman at her formal prom in a short satin dress and gauntlet gloves

Teens at a formal dance

1940's Style Guide | 29

The Teenager

The term 'teenager' was first coined in 1944, around the time Seventeen Magazine printed its first issue, showing off young styles for teenage girls. Teenagers didn't want to dress like their mothers, and adopted styles to set them apart from the older crowd. They were obsessed with crooner Frank Sinatra, hung out at soda fountains and danced all night to jazz and swing music.

The most popular teenage look of the '40s was the "Sloppy Joe" sweater. It was a plain crew-neck or cardigan sweater, worn slightly too big by teenage girls. They wore a white blouse underneath with a pointed or small, rounded peter pan collar peeking out of the top. The blouse was tucked into a plaid or plain pleated skirt with the un-tucked sweater over it. Teenagers' skirts were made of rayon, wool blends or wool and zipped or buttoned on the side. They could be grey, tan or blue, red or green plaid. The skirt was a little bit longer and fuller than those adult women wore. The outfit was completed with a pair of white bobby socks, or cotton, ankle-length socks.

Another popular outfit for younger girls was a plain cotton shirtwaist dress with a short-sleeved cotton linen or rayon jacket over it. The jacket could be worn buttoned up or open and had shoulder pads. It fell between the waist and hipline, and usually the dress and jacket were not the same color. The dress was plain, plaid or checked. Reds and blues were popular colors, and the jacket was a coordinating color.

Teenagers also wore plain short-sleeved cotton blouses tucked into a gathered rayon, wool-blend or wool skirts. The skirt came to just below the knees and was gathered a little bit to give it some swing. Teens' skirts were often plaid, but could also be plain navy, red, blue or grey, among other colors.

Cotton dresses and sweaters

Plaid skirt, white blouse, oxford shoes

Swing dancing

Wedding Dresses

Although the world was in turmoil during the '40s, people still got married! In fact, so many people did during the years immediately after the war that the Baby Boom exploded. However, weddings were not as formal as they had been before or would be after the decade. Quite often the bride, groom and wedding party would all wear their best suits or dresses. Some brides chose to make a new dress for the occasion with a color and design that was wearable after the wedding. Rose pink was a popular choice for both brides and bridesmaids. While silk and satin were unavailable during the war, lace and tulle were not rationed, but were very expensive. In the U.S., rayon satin, crepe and taffeta were made available for sale as a way to boost morale during the tough times. After the war, white silk parachutes were released for sale back to the public and quickly became choice materials for both wedding dresses and bridal lingerie.

Brides often wore their mothers' wedding dresses or dresses worn by other close friends or family members. Many used these old wedding dresses to create a new design, or wore them as is. In some larger cities, renting a wedding dress was an option. The shortage of wedding dresses was especially felt in the UK, where it wasn't uncommon for dresses to be brought over from the USA, and then worn at by at least a dozen brides in the next year.

Betty and Ray Bukovnik married in her best suit and white peep toe pumps, her groom wore a pinstripe double breasted suit

Ray and Betty Bukovnick's wedding party all wearing their best dresses and suits

If the bride was a uniformed servicewoman she usually wore her best uniform since she did not have civilian rationing stamps to purchase wedding clothes. A serviceman groom also wore his best uniform for the wedding day, or his most formal suit, usually double- breasted in blue or grey.

For those who could afford to make or buy a wedding dress, the styles were similar to day dresses. They always had long sleeves and full skirts, but the "princess" look was not achievable with the fabric restrictions of the period. Dresses usually had a sweetheart neckline and fitted bodice with fitted sleeves that were slightly gathered or puffed at the shoulder. From the waist, a circle skirt fell to the floor possibly with a short train. Dresses were rather plain, missing any intricate embroidery or beading. The decoration and attention went to the veil and headpiece. Brides always wore a long single layer net veil, often attached to a little pillbox hat pinned to the head. A headband of seasonal flowers was another popular piece, with or without a veil. The flowers on the headband matched the bride and groom's corsages and the bride's very large bouquet. A white pearl necklace was the sole piece of jewelry worn by nearly every bride in the 1940s.

Bridesmaids, if they dressed up, wore similar dresses to the bride, often with short sleeves. Bridesmaids' dresses were a light shade of blue, green, pink or a pretty floral print, and bridesmaids often wore shorter veils, hats and flowers in their hair.

A homemade wedding dress made from post war recycled silk parachute

Catalog wedding gown, bridesmaids dress and flower girl dress.

The Rebel Girls

Although the man's Zoot Suit is more well-known, young women also participated in the rebellious Zoot and Zazou style. Their version of the Zoot Suit was a short pleated skirt, sitting at the natural waist, that showed plenty of leg, hemmed an inch or two above the knee! The skirt was made of rayon or cotton and was gathered to swing for all of that dancing. It was usually plain but brightly colored, and fastened on the side with a metal zipper or buttons. A plain white blouse, usually short-sleeved, was worn tucked into the skirt.

Women also wore a wide, long wool suit jacket with large shoulder pads, worn almost as long as their skirts. Fishnet or striped stockings or knee socks were worn with black leather thick soled, 2 ½-inch high, high-heeled shoes with an ankle strap. For the Latina Zoot-suiter, hair was worn in a giant, exaggerated bouffant-style on top of the head with the rest of the hair falling loose in the back. The French Zazou's hair was worn long and curly and dyed platinum blond. Girls in the Zoot Suit movement all wore heavy makeup.

The New Look

After World War II was over, in 1947, Parisian designer Christian Dior sent his debut collection down the runway. His creations, dubbed the "New Look", by a Vogue columnist, were the antithesis of wartime fashions. While wartime clothes had been plain and straight, the New Look featured a voluptuous hourglass figure with an accentuated bust and hips and a tiny "wasp waist". The bodice was tight and the shoulders were soft and sloping, rather than square and padded. The skirts were gigantic, puffed up with tulle, and long, coming to mid-calf. The fabrics used were luxurious silks, taffetas and wools, and a lot of them, as almost 20 yards of fabric were gathered and pleated to make each skirt. The extreme hourglass look was achieved by padding the bust and hips, and wearing a corset around the waist to force the curvaceous silhouette.

Although the "New Look" was very well received by fashion critics, many women were slow to adopt it into their wardrobes, particularly in the United States. Protests even went on in America, from Dallas to Chicago to New York. After the austerity of the war, women felt that the excessive use of fabric was an insult to all of the scraping and saving that they had done. They had stopped wearing restrictive undergarments and had gotten used to wearing clothes that could be lived in, whether for work, housework or play. The "New Look" was as cumbersome and as impractical as it gets, and women saw it as moving backward instead of forward.

Dior's New Look

1940's Style Guide 33

Although women weren't interested in the "New Look" quite yet, they were ready for a change. The war was hard on everyone, and women wanted some luxury back in their lives, while still holding on to the practicality and freedom gained in clothing during the war. A modified version of the style became fashionable in the late '40s in the U.S. Shoulder pads got smaller and the waists of jackets and dresses became more exaggerated, but still didn't require corsets. Skirts became slightly fuller, some with pleating, and hemlines got longer too, most people adopting the new mid-calf length. A popular "New Look" style in the U.S. was a tightly fitted bodice with a fuller, flared skirt, minus the corsets and tulle underskirts of the real, Parisian "New Look". The full "New Look," much like that from the Paris runway, would eventually be adopted by everyone, and became the reigning style of the 1950s.

A 1950's party dress
Timelessvixen.com

Right: The shirtwaist dress continues to be a classic dress, even today

Women's accessories

Shoes

What outfit could be complete without the perfect pair of shoes? In the 1940s shoes were, like everything else, very practical. Although the U.S. avoided ration coupons for clothing by placing restrictions like L-85 on manufacturers, leather was greatly needed to make boots for soldiers and leather shoes became the only clothing item that was rationed.

Heels were short, typically only an inch or two, and thicker than today's heels, measuring about a half inch to an inch square. Most heels were stacked, and in the very late '40s, a slight platform

Wedge sling back shoes
Hollyvoguevintage.com

was popular. Wedge heels were also worn and were about the same height. Shoes were a little bit chunky by today's standards, and the front was very blunt and rounded. In the U.S., some shoes were peep-toes and had a very, very small opening that did not reveal much of the toes.

Peep Toe Mesh Pumps
Simplicityisblis (etsy.com)

34 1940's Style Guide

Leather shoes were still available, of course, but the supply was limited. Regular leather, patent leather and suede were all used frequently for shoes, even during the war years. Colors for leather were also limited, and most shoe styles were only available in a few choices. Black, brown, tan, white and navy were the most popular and widely available, along with a burgundy-brown shade. A lot of people bought rubber soles to attach to the bottoms of their leather-soled shoes to reduce wear and make them last longer, or allow the soles to be replaced the following year if necessary. If you didn't have enough ration stamps for new shoes, you had to make do!

Since leather wasn't readily available, shoes were made from alternate materials during the war. Although most women preferred leather shoes, stores and catalogues started advertising "ration-free" shoes, made out of cloth and wood. Straw and cotton canvas were used for shoe uppers intended for warm-weather wear. The bottoms of shoes could be made from rubber or other plastics, but those materials were also in short supply. Some shoe bottoms were made out of wood, but this was both uncomfortable and impractical, since the shoes were heavy and hard to walk in. Plus, if you wore them out in the rain they had to be dried properly or the wood would split, ruining the shoes!

Peep toe shoes

Navy mesh peep toe shoes
Kickshaw (etsy.com)

Oxford wedges
Remixvintageshoes.com

Slingback sandals
Mbellishedbloom (etsy.com)

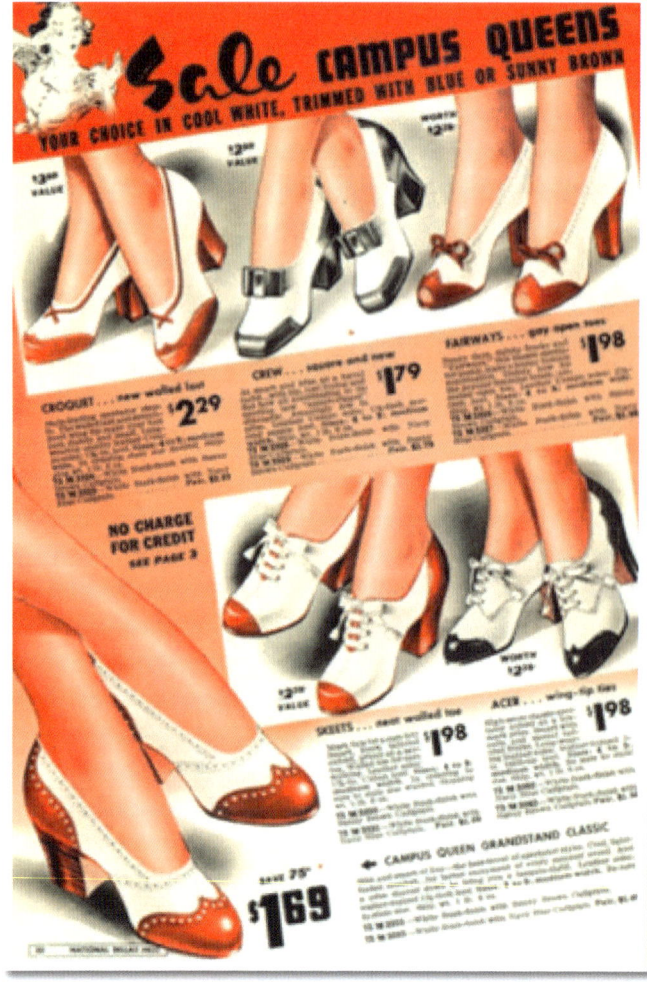

1940's Style Guide 35

There were only a few popular styles of shoes in the '40s. For daywear, the oxford could be worn with anything. The shoe was closed with a short, thick heel and front lacing, much like a classic men's dress shoe. Oxfords were sometimes decorated with perforations on the sides. The sling-back shoe was also a daywear staple, with a rounded front, sometimes with a small peep-toe opening, and a strap attached with a buckle around the back of the ankle. Heels ranged in width and height and could make the shoe more or less casual. Regular pumps were worn, in the same style as the sling-back. Pumps and sling-backs were often decorated with various types of bows attached onto the front of the shoe, and could also be decorated with perforations, like an oxford. All of these could be worn with a wedge heel, instead of a stacked heel.

During the summer, straw wedge espadrilles were practical and stylish, with a closed or open toe and ankle straps. For evening, shoes often had a crossed front in a pump style or had a strap around the ankle. Teenagers wore saddle shoes and penny loafers. Saddle shoes were white lace-up oxford style shoes with a darker colored panel in the middle of the shoe, usually in black or navy, with no heel. Penny loafers were a flat slip-on with a large tongue in the front of the shoe, and a slot on the front where a penny was placed.

1942 saddle shoes

Suede pumps
Pranceandswagger (etsy.com)

Platform Pumps

Remixvintageshoes.com

Summer wedges and oxfords with peep toes

1940's Style Guide

Vintage, Reproduction or New Shoes?

When it comes choosing a pair of shoes for your 1940s outfit, both style and comfort are critical. Vintage shoes offer style, but not always comfort. Women's feet in the 1940s were narrower, and finding your size can be a big challenge. If you do find your size, you may notice the lack of cushioning, especially in heels. Women were used to less comfortable shoes then, and their feet could handle more than our feet today. Some women are disgusted by the thought of wearing someone else's used shoes. If this is you, then you do not want to wear vintage shoes, unless they are dead stock, or shoes that were never sold or worn.

Recently, a few companies have started to make 1940s reproduction shoes. Although they can be fairly pricey, the comfort and authentic style is ideal if you are doing reenactments or other events that require period accuracy. These shoes are available in a wide variety of sizes and sometimes even various widths.

http://www.remixvintageshoes.com/
-Reproduction vintage shoes at their best

http://www.allaboutdance.com/
-Carries Aris Alen 1940s Dance shoes; non- dancers will love these too

Sandals, wedges and oxfords

http://www.swinggear.co.uk/
-In the UK, look here for 1940s dance shoes

http://www.rocketoriginals.co.uk/
-(UK) Reproduction shoes for men and women

http://www.american-duchess.com/
- Historical footwear

You can also wear modern shoes. Luckily, shoes styles have not changed much in the last 100 years, so finding 1940s-style shoes is not difficult. Once you know what style to look for almost any shoe store should have something that will work for you. If you prefer to shop online, I have compiled a shopping page of stores that offer 1940s-style modern shoes:

http://www.vintagedancer.com/1940s/1940s-womens-shoes/
-New 1940s style shoes

Some of my favorite modern online shoes stores are:

http://www.payless.com/store/
-Carries wedges and Mary Jane shoes locally and online

http://www.shoebuy.com/
-Many great choices with sometimes better prices then other sites

http://www.modcloth.com/
Very cute vintage inspired shoes

Hats

Hats weren't rationed or restricted during the war, and women wore them in a wide range of styles to dress up their plain, unadorned outfits. The hat wasn't a necessary accessory, but it was worn with suits, rayon dresses and even eveningwear. As far as style and design, the sky was the limit when it came to hats, and they ranged from wearable and practical to frivolous and playful.

The plain beret came in a variety of colors, typically made from wool or rayon felt. It was worn either on the side of the head on an angle, or straight on top and pushed towards the back of the head. Berets were worn with more casual dresses and suits.

1944 flower clip hat and earrings

1940's Style Guide

The pillbox hat was also worn a lot during the '40s. It was stiff and round, with feathers, bows and often a net veil that covered the eyes. Pillbox hats were worn on top of the head or at an angle on the side of the head. Hat pins held the hat in place. The pillbox hat could be worn with anything, from daywear to evening gowns, depending upon the style of the hat.

The practical turban was a staple of the '40s wardrobe and could be worn with anything, from suits to day dresses to evening gowns. Turbans were also popular for the working girl, since they kept the hair safe and secure so that it wouldn't get caught in factory machines or get dirty. Turbans were made from a variety of materials, depending on their use, and came in a rainbow of colors. For work-wear, cotton or rayon was the material of choice. Rayon was also used for casual daywear turbans, while fancy ones were made from rayon velvet. More elegant styles also featured bows or other decorations on the top.

Miniature hats and flower clips were exceedingly popular in the '40s. They often had brims, and could be round or flat on top. These hats were made from felt or straw and were decorated with feathers, ribbons, bows, flowers and beads. Some featured a net veil in the front that covered the eyes, or even the entire face. The hats were pinned on with hat pins, and were often worn at a jaunty, fun angle.

http://www.vintagehatbox.com/
– Vintage hats, hat boxes, hat pins, gloves and more
http://www.villagehatshop.com/womens-hats.html
– Modern hats but some with vintage style : Beret, Pill Box, Veiled and Turban hats
http://www.amazon.com/gp/product/1934268941
– How to Make Hats and Accessories: Instructions for Making 1940s Fashions book
http://www.amazon.com/gp/product/1934268631?
– Vintage instruction guide for making 1940s Hats
http://www.wearinghistorypatterns.com/1940s-wwii-victory-hat-pattern/
– Pattern for two WW2 era hats

Straw hat with felt trim and grossgrain ribbon

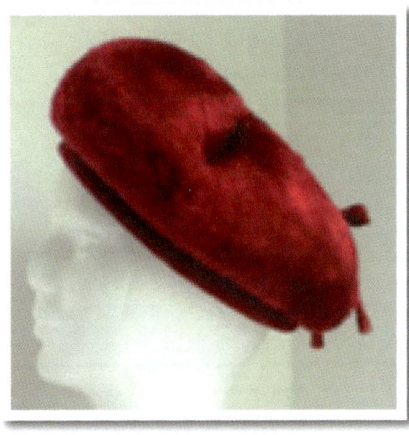

Red faux fur felt beret with bow

1948 small saucer shaped straw hats called Sailor hats

Blue felt hat with chiffon bow band

Pillbox hat with veil

Floppy summer hat with velvet bow

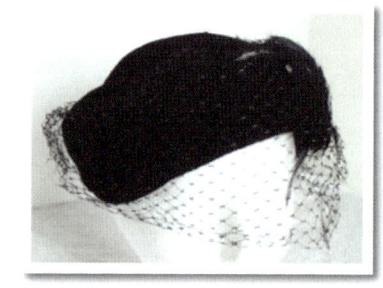

Black velvet small hat with feather and veil

Original 1940s knit turban pattern and hat made by https://www.facebook.com/pages/1940s-Style-For-You/

Bags

There were a few styles of bags that were widely used for both day and evening in the '40s. The strapped handbag was usually made from leather or patent leather, although the new forms of plastic were also used as imitation materials. Women made handbags at home from fabric, often in bright colors, but most strapped handbags for daytime use were black, brown or white. Bags were smaller than those carried by women today, typically less than 12 inches wide. They were rectangular or fan-shaped with a single thin shoulder strap that reached down to the hip when worn and closed with a metal clasp at the top of the bag. Others had a shorter single strap of no more than a foot long that was simply held in the hand. These closed by folding over the top to a snap. Fan-shaped bags were gathered at the top, giving them a slightly different look than the smooth rectangular handbags. Bags were generally plain and undecorated.

Evening bags closely resembled these daytime shoulder bags, except they were smaller and made of different materials. Evening bags were made of silky rayon or rayon velvet, and were often decorated with beads. The strap was short and colors were more varied for evening bags, often matching or coordinating with the dress and shoes.

Brown leather purse
Snap-it-upvintageclothing.com

1940's Style Guide 39

Clutch-style purses were used for both day and evening. These were rectangular and about the same size as the strapped bags. They were very flat and used a fold-over snap closure, often with a button for decoration. Clutches were commonly made in leather, patent leather and plastic imitation materials.

A craze for woven plastic purses swept the nation in the mid-forties. Popular styles were rectangular clutches and fan shapes either with straps or in clutch form. These were similar in style to the other bags except they were made from plastic that was woven to look like a crocheted or woven material. Fan shaped bags from woven plastic were not gathered. Woven plastic handbags came in any number of bright colors and sizes.

The box bag was used often as well, and looked much like it sounds it would. The bags were small and geometric, available in a variety of shapes, including circles, rectangles and six or eight sided shapes in box form. They had a small strap or two small straps attached to the top and held in the hand. These bags were made from leather, patent leather and plastic, often in black or brown. Some had a top that came off, while others were attached and fastened on the side with a metal clasp.

http://www.retrodesignerdeals.com/
– A nice collection of vintage handbags and other accessories
http://www.pursestreet.com/
– Stunning collection but not organized by decade

Crocodile embossed handbag
Snap-it-upvintageclothing.com

Suede box purse
Cookiekvintage (etsy.com)

Gold chain mesh purse
Memeworld

Box purse
Hollyvoguevintage.com

Woven plastic clutch
5anddimememories (etsy.com)

Beaded bronze purse
Thevintagemistress (etsy.com)

Gloves

Gloves were definitely optional during the '40s, and fewer women wore them everyday. Working in and outside of the home and a trend towards more casual, practical clothing caused many to go bare-handed all of the time. However, some women still wore gloves during the day. Daytime gloves were usually made from leather or suede in dark, neutral colors like navy, tan, brown and black, although dark red and green were also used. Elbow-length gloves were pushed down towards the wrists or wrist-length gloves were worn.

Although not an evening necessity, gloves were worn more for dressy occasions than for daily wear. White or ivory wrist-length gloves made of rayon were worn with nicer day dresses to dress them up. For evening, shiny or matte rayon elbow-length gloves were worn in a variety of colors to match the dress and were often shirred to add interest.

Glove Patterns
Sovintagepatterns.com

Beaded Evening Gloves
Hautemamavintage (etsy.com)

Jewelry

Jewelry in the 1940s was big and often colorful, adding character to plain outfits. Fashion jewelry was made from inexpensive metals, including silver, and other materials like plastic, Lucite and enamel.. Rhinestones took the place of precious stones. Jewelry designs were often sculptural, featuring ribbons, flowers and animals

Beaded necklaces were popular during the day. They came in a variety of shapes, but many were round beads chained together. Both pearls and faux pearls were worn. Beads used for necklaces were usually large, or strands of smaller beads could be braided together or worn together to form a multi-strand necklace. Beads were plastic, Lucite or glass and were available in any and every color. Necklaces were usually worn at a medium length, about 16 inches, to mid-chest.

Flower pin brooch
mimisvintageshop (etsy.com)

1940's Style Guide 41

Earrings often matched the necklace, but did not always. They usually had a post screw-on backing of silver with colorful plastic, Lucite or glass attached on the front. Earrings were sculptural, like other jewelry and were often round in shape and quite large – maybe ½-inch to an inch in diameter. They were very three-dimensional, with beads and rhinestones formed into flower-like shapes.

Both identification bracelets and charm bracelets were popular in the '40s. ID bracelets were a thin metal chain with a metal rectangle attached in the center. Made from both gold and silver, most identification bracelets were a gold tone. The center plate had the person's name engraved on it, often in cursive-style writing. Charm bracelets were thin gold or silver chains, more often silver, with different charms attached at intervals. Women and girls collected the charms to fill up their bracelets. They could be anything from flowers and animals to lucky horseshoes and clovers. Bells, hearts and household items were also made into charms, and charms could be used to show off the personality and likes of the wearer.

Bead necklace
Memeworld (etsy.com)

Silver rose necklace
Jewelspeak (etsy.com)

Rhinestone jewelry
Hollyvoguevintage.com

Flower brooch
Treasuredtimespast (etsy.com)

1940's Style Guide

Brooches are not worn often today, but in the '40s they were worn all the time, attached to suit lapels and on the chests of dresses and blouses. They were colorful and had lots of character to them. Literally, anything could end up the subject of a brooch in the '40s. Popular shapes included flowers, animals and ribbons, all three-dimensional. Patriotic brooches were worn to show support for the war, including those in the shape of soldiers, planes and red, white and blue 'V's for victory. Brooches were made from plastic, enamel, Lucite and colored rhinestones with silver straight pin backs. Young women often wore military insignia pins given to them as presents by their soldier boyfriends stationed overseas.

For evening, clear rhinestones were a favorite. Necklaces, bracelets and earrings were usually a set. Geometric and flower shapes were popular instead of strands of stones or beads. Evening jewelry wasn't dainty, and necklaces and bracelets were wide, often set with large stones. Evening earrings, unlike daytime ones, often dangled from the earlobe, but were still usually post-backed.

www.michellesvintagejewelry.com
– A diverse collection of 1940s jewelry
www.earthlyadornments.com
– Sorted by decade. Quality Jewelry
www.morninggloryantiques.com
– Some very unique pieces in this huge collection
www.penelopespearls.com
– Look under "Retro Modern" for 1940s pieces
www.gaslightshadows.com
– Not an online store but if you're visiting San Francisco be sure to check here for Bakelite jewelry

Charm Bracelet
Jewelspeak (etsy.com)

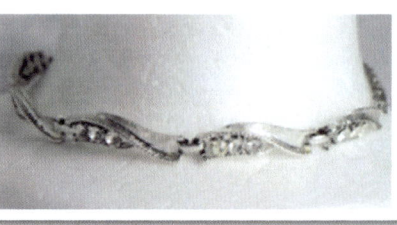

My grandmother's formal rhinestone and silver necklace

Rhinestone Earrings
mimisvintageshop (etsy.com)

Colorful costume earrings

Double strand bead necklace

The underwear

Lingerie

When people think of 1940s lingerie, they usually think of the glamorous, curvy, satin and lace pin-up girls whose pictures filled the magazines popular with lonely soldiers overseas, beautiful women posed provocatively in corsets, nightgowns and swimsuits with a look that remains iconic today.

The reality, however, was quite different. Women back home were not lounging around in fancy, restrictive undergarments. They were enjoying a new freedom working and being active outside, and because of wartime shortages in materials, they also enjoyed a new freedom in their undergarments. In the 1930s, women were still wearing metal-boned corsets, but new technology soon allowed for girdles to take the place of corsets. Elastic fabrics were fashioned into tight-fitting, full-body girdles that sucked and smoothed every lump and bump. The '30s full-body version of the girdle included a bra top attached to a very short skirt with elasticized straps with metal fasteners to attach to silk stockings. Remember, up until the '60s, stockings were worn without a top or panty. They came up to mid-thigh and had to be held up with straps attached to a garter belt or girdle. Bras were not very advanced – cup sizes were first invented in 1935 and underwires in 1938. In the late 1930s, the rubber girdle was introduced. It really was made out of rubber and was covered in 'breathing' holes for ventilation.

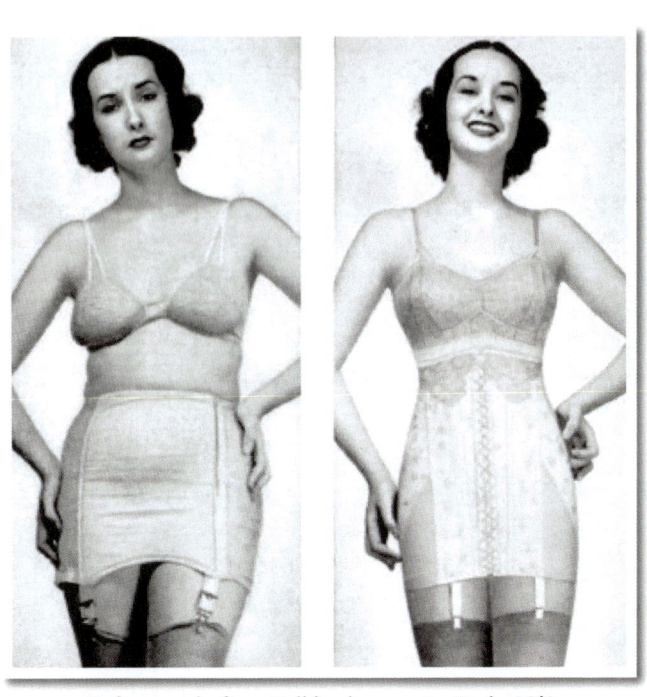

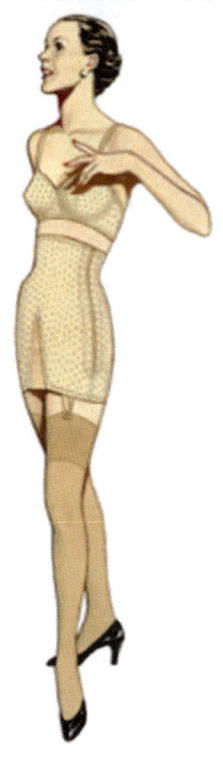

Before and after: Full body corset - Early 40'S

1940's Underwear
Dover Clip Art

1940's Style Guide

The war affected undergarments, just as it affected all other aspects of dress. Production of the new rubber girdles came to a halt because rubber was needed for the war. The same went for corsets, as the steel used for the boning was needed. This was an advantage for women who required more flexibility and movement with their new lifestyles.

The brassiere became shortened to the 'bra' in the '40s. Bras of the era were plain without lace or decoration, and were most frequently made from rayon satin or cotton. They were usually white, ivory or the very popular peachy-pink. Straps were adjustable and the bras fastened at the back with metal hooks and eyes, just like today's bras. The shape of '40s bras was very different. They covered much more and created a different look than the bras of today. All bras were full-coverage, with the underwire reaching all the way from one side to the other and many did not have underwires. There was a substantial amount of fabric in the center, creating separation between the breasts, instead of the pushed-together cleavage of today. The straps came from the middle of the cups, rather than the sides. Bras usually came below the bust, covering some torso, and the shape they created was pointier than today, because the bra cups had several seams on them that came together at a point. Bras of the 1940s, while pointy, did not have the exaggerated pointy "Bullet Bra" look of the '50s.

Panties were not really worn by women until the 1930s, but became more popular in the '40s. The panties of the '40s would put even today's 'granny panties' to shame. They were made from rayon satin or cotton in colors similar to those used for bras and were quite plain. They were not close-fitting or small, reaching up past the belly button and looking more like shorts than a bikini bottom, and most came down a few inches on the legs. Talk about coverage!

Although girdles couldn't be made in the same way that they were in the '30s, they were produced and worn throughout the '40s. They were made with rayon or cotton, and a small amount of elastic was used to give them some stretch. They usually had elastic panels on the front and back, the rest of the fabric was flat, woven and rigid. The girdle was very tight to suck everything in, and began above the waistline. It came down into a skirt to cover the backside completely and had four elastic straps with metal clips to attach stockings.

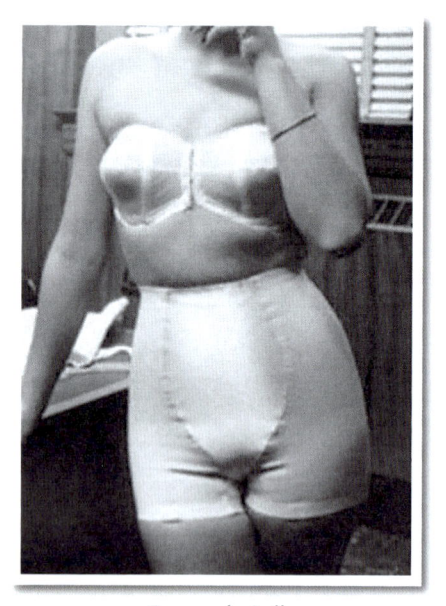

Bra and girdle

Panties
Beeskneesclothing (etsy.com)

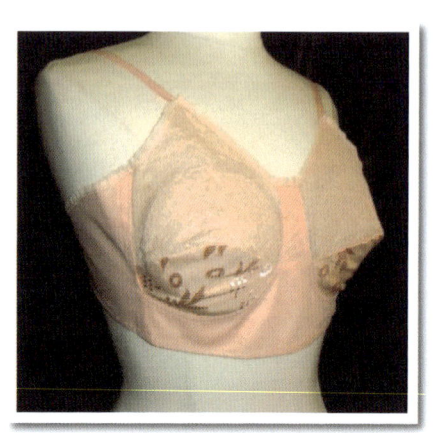

Peach pink bra
Sewingmachinegirl (etsy.com)

Dress slip
Retrowardrobe.com

1940's Style Guide   45

Since many women were wearing pants, a new type of "panty girdle" was introduced to the market. It was the same thing as a standard girdle, except it took the form of a panty instead of a skirt. Girdles usually fastened with metal zippers on one side. Although girdles offered a smooth shape underneath the new closer-fitting clothes, many women chose not to wear them at all during the decade, wearing just a bra and panties for the first time.

Slips were the last underwear layer a lady needed to create the perfect shape and preserve her modesty. Slips came in long dress-like varieties or shorter skirt and top only selections. Slips were usually white or soft peachy pink, with thin shoulder straps and a figure flattering shape. No dress, suit or skirt would be complete without a slip to keep clothing from clinging to your body, and in the case of rayon dresses, keep your legs from showing through the fabric.

www.curvaceousbeauties.com
– Vintage modern plus size lingerie
www.slipland.net
– Vintage slips to go with your vintage dresses
www.girdlebound.com
– Girdles of course
www.whatkatiedid.us.com
– Vintage reproduction lingerie, stockings, corsets and more

1945 lingerie ad in Vanity Fair

Modern Girdles - Advice For Creating The 1940'S Shape

It is critical when wearing vintage or 1940s reproduction clothing to create the proper shape. The 40s shape was all about small waists, rounded bosoms, and full hips. It is known as the "natural" women's shape, although if you ask most women there is nothing natural about it. Natural women have far too many bumps and curves to create the hourglass 40s shape without a little help. You can buy vintage girdles, bras, slips and panties from a variety of offline and online sources, but if you don't have the time or budget to go the authentic route, there are modern undergarments that can create a similar effect and may be more comfortable than a retro-style girdle.

Most lingerie stores carry full body shape wear and half body tummy tuckers. These work nicely to create the correct silhouette, just try them on first and choose the ones that tighten your waist and smooth your tummy the most. High-waisted "control top" nylons can also help smooth your bumps a little or a pair of Spanx, or a similar modern shaper, can really suck things in. If you want to make your own full body shaper without the cost of a brand new one, you can buy a pair of control top nylons that are 2-3 sizes bigger than your normal nylon size. Put on the nylons pulling them all the way up to your bra or over it if you need a little "minimizing." Cut off the legs at just above the knee, and you have an instant body shaper.

I must emphasize that it is very critical that you wear proper shaping undergarments, or else vintage dresses look frumpy and fit poorly. Take your measurements wearing appropriate undergarments before buying clothing. The measurement difference could be subtle or quite dramatic, depending on your body shaper. Reproduction dresses and vintage modern styles tend to be tailored to modern bodies and therefore may not need shaping undergarments.

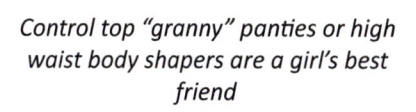

Control top "granny" panties or high waist body shapers are a girl's best friend

Hosiery

Before the 1940s, women would not leave the house without wearing a pair of silk stockings. In fact, it was not considered appropriate to be bare-legged in public whatsoever, unless you were at the beach. Silk stockings came up to mid-thigh and had to be held up with garters attached to corsets, girdles or a garter belt. Before the late '30s, fabrics were not elasticized, so they were not stretchy at all. Once nylon was invented, stockings were made from that instead of costlier and more delicate silk. Stockings were sheer and nude colored, but darker than the skin, and had seams up the backs and at the backs of the ankles where they were sewn together.

During the war, all silk and nylon went to the war effort and stockings became a precious commodity. They snagged and tore easily, and it was hard to keep a pair around for long. Women had to conserve their stockings for very special occasions, and fought over any that might be available for purchase. Most of the time, they had no choice but to go bare-legged. The government went so far as to ask churches to tell women it was alright to attend without stockings.

Women began to stain their legs with brown household items like gravy browning, coffee and cocoa powder to give the appearance of stockings. Soon enough leg cosmetics were born that stained the legs a tan color, sort of the first self-tanners. The first versions stained dresses and ran off in the rain, but newer versions were better, and came in liquid, cream or powder that was mixed with water. Several different shades were offered to complement different skin tones. All of the makeup companies, like Max Factor and Elizabeth Arden, got on board. Some women took it a step further, and drew a stocking seam on the backs of their legs with brown or black eyebrow or eyeliner pencil, often enlisting the help of a friend to get it straight. After the war, nylon stockings returned and women went right back to wearing them, attached to garters on girdles or garter belts.

Socks were not often worn by women, but white ankle socks were very popular with teenage girls. They were worn with saddle shoes or penny loafers. White or black socks were also worn by many women working in factories for comfort and protection.

1940's Style Guide 47

Sleepwear

Sleepwear in the '40s was simple and practical. Since a lot of men were overseas, most women didn't have to worry about what they wore to bed, as no one would see them anyway! Women wore nightgowns in cotton, cotton flannel, rayon and rayon satin. They also had a bedjacket or robe to put over the nightgown before bed and in the morning.

Some nightgowns looked like a slip, and were made of rayon or rayon satin that flowed nicely over the body. These were usually ankle-length and were fitted in the bodice and flared out to an A-line shaped skirt. These nightgowns had a low V-neck that was often decorated with lace and were usually sleeveless or had thin straps, but also sometimes had very short sleeves. An empire waist was popular – there was stitching or lace underneath the bustline and the skirt of the nightgown began from this line, rather than the natural waist. Soft colors were popular, including white, ivory, light pink and light blue.

Many women chose comfort over style in their sleepwear, choosing nightgowns in cotton or warmer cotton flannel. These were looser, made without a defined waist. They could be sleeveless, have short cap sleeves, or have long sleeves for warmth. More casual nightgowns like this were sometimes decorated with lace or eyelet at the neck and sleeves. Soft colors and floral patterns were common. Sleeved nightgowns often buttoned up the front to a high, rounded collar. Sleeveless ones could button up the back and have a rounded or v neckline. Cotton nightgowns could be mid-calf or ankle length.

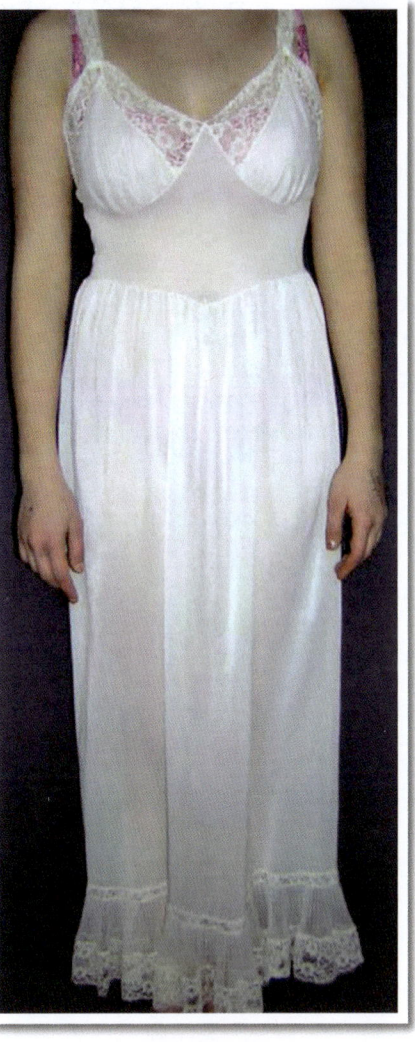

Nightgown
Retrowardrobe.com

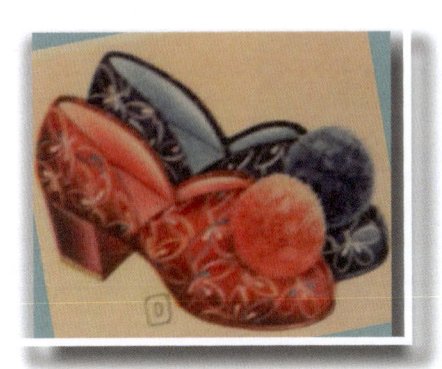

Bedroom Slippers

Rare pajama set
snap-it-uptvintageclothing (etsy.com)

Bed jacket
Hollyvoguevintage.com

1940's Style Guide

Bedjackets were a nighttime staple in the '40s. They were worn around the house over a nightgown for both warmth and modesty. The bedjacket style of the time was a cropped jacket with elbow-length sleeves. It was about waist-length or a little longer. The jacket was cut straight and was loose fitting through the body and sleeves. While elbow-length sleeves were most popular, sleeves could also be short or long. These jackets tied around the neck with a ribbon, closed with one button in the center, or buttoned all the way down. They could be cotton or rayon satin, and were often quilted, but some were knitted. Popular colors were white, pale pink, peach and light blue.

Robes were worn for the same purposes as bed jackets, except they were floor length, and usually made from cotton, cotton flannel or quilted rayon satin. Robes were loose-fitting and cut straight, and sleeves were usually the same way. Some had a small stand-up collar while others had folded-over lapels. They usually tied with a sash at the waist, and many had two large pockets at arm's length in the front. Most robes had long sleeves that were gathered and slightly puffed, and some even had shoulder pads. Colors for robes were often darker and richer for winter wear, including burgundy, navy, dark-toned plaids and florals.

http://www.silverscreenloungerie.com/ – Nightgowns, slips, dressing gowns and bed jackets from the 30s, 40s, and 50s

1944 quilted robe

The beauty

Both women and notions of female beauty really have come a long way in the last several decades. One read through some beauty tips from the '40s will make you realize that! Some of the advice women followed was downright insulting, some simply wrong, and believe it or not, some is still followed today!

In the '40s, women were told that although they most likely weren't naturally pretty, since so few women were, they could make themselves presentable using corrective makeup and hairstyling. To be naturally beautiful, you had to have clear skin, sparkling eyes, a perfectly symmetrical and oval shaped face, good posture, excellent grooming, personal style and a "natural goodness". Whew! If you couldn't meet all of these qualifications you could do some things to fix yourself up, and even women over 40 were told to make sure they never became dowdy.

The first step to perfecting your face is to improve the skin. Apparently almost no women over 25 had normal skin, at least according to beauty advice. According to women's magazines of the 40s, after 25, skin either became overly dry or oily. To combat dry skin, it was recommended to use soaps with expensive ingredients and secret formulas for dry skin. Sounds pricey! Soft water was essential, whether from a water softener, distilled water or fresh rain water she had collected herself. After removing makeup with the specialty soap and water, cleansing cream was massaged into the face. Oily skin was a whole different matter, and one said to cause misery.

1940's Style Guide   49

While we know that it's very normal today, in the '40s, oily skin was thought to be caused by a medical problem. Women with oily skin might be over or underweight, have a poor diet, be constipated, stressed, have poor posture or a 'mental disturbance.' They were told to correct these internal problems in order to fix their oily skin, by dieting, exercising, relaxing or seeing a psychologist. Deep breathing and warm baths were also recommended to relieve stress, open pores and increase elimination. Once the mental disturbance was managed, soap and water cleansed the face, but women were instructed to make sure to massage all of the oil out of it for several minutes, followed by astringent lotion and/or calamine lotion. Rain water, naturally, is best for oily skin.

If a woman had a problem with blackheads (and really, who doesn't?), she could take warm baths to open up pores, rinse her face with warm water followed by cold, and scrub her face twice a day with a rough washcloth or facial brush. Blackhead extractors were used religiously to keep pores clear.

Before the age of Botox wrinkles were simply a fact of life. However, massaging the face was thought to prevent them, and slathering vegetable oil or all-purpose cream was another wrinkle remedy. Wrinkle-repair has become so high-tech since then!

Of course, an essential part of a woman's beauty in the '40s was keeping a trim figure (must be easy on those rations!) Weight loss, called 'reducing' at the time, was actually fairly straightforward, and the methods used really do hold true today. To reduce, women followed a low calorie, low fat, and low carb diet, avoiding salt and getting plenty of vitamins and minerals. They were also encouraged to chew food well, keep their bowels active and drink eight glasses of water a day. Unlike today, they routinely reduced food intake in proportion to the amount of alcohol drank per day.

Hair

It was important to keep hair clean and shiny, washing it whenever necessary. Women massaged their scalps and brushed their hair twice a day. When shampoos became scarce, and of poor quality, women had to steam their hair over a pot of hot water and then rub the dirt and oil off with a towel.

In the '40s women were encouraged to use their hair to 'fix' any flaws in their face. If you had perfect, shiny hair with a good color, you should use it to frame your face. If you had a full or round face, magazines recommended hairstyles that piled hair on top of your head to distract from it. If a thin face was your problem, your hairstyle should be down and over your ears to make it look wider.

Hair was usually worn shoulder-length or slightly longer, and cut straight with no bangs. Specific hairstyles, especially with waving, required different haircuts. Women's hair was usually worn in the same style every day, until she went to the salon to have it re-cut and restyled. There were several popular hairstyles during

Even confined to a relocation camp these Japanese-American women pin curled their hair every night, styling with water and homemade products

the '40s, but they all had a few things in common. First, they were all perfectly styled, without any sort of messiness or undone quality. Second, they were never, ever straight and sleek. Curls and volume were essential. Hairdos almost always started with pin-curls and were styled from there. Following are some tips you can use to recreate a perfect '40s hairstyle.

Tip: The essential styling products you need to create a 40s 'do: Styling Lotion (such as Lottabody, found in the ethnic hair product section,) pomade, hair spray, bobby pins and long U-shaped hair pins.

1940's Style Guide

Achieving pin-curls takes some effort and practice, but they were an everyday process for women in the '40s, set at night and styled the next morning. You'll need to start after washing your hair at night or misting it with water until damp. Let hair air dry until it's just damp and then start the curls. Take about a ½-inch to an inch-wide section of hair and twist it around your finger from end to root. Slide the hair off of your finger so that it lays flat on your head in a circle and pin it in place with two hair pins or bobby pins forming an X-shape with the pins. Repeat with additional sections of hair until your whole head is done. Make sure to twirl the curls in the same direction, or in the direction you want them to curl when taken down. Tie a scarf around your head so that your hair is fully covered and then go to sleep! It may be uncomfortable, but that's the price you'll have to pay for perfect pin-curls. In the morning, take the pins out and fix the curls so that they lay properly before styling. If you are in a hurry you can apply low hot heat with the hairdryer over your pin curls, but sleeping on the pincurls is much better for your hair and less frizzy.

After performing this ritual once you'll see why permanent waves became so popular during the '40s!

http://youtu.be/6PBwSXHWvA8
– Pin Curl Video Tutorial

The easiest '40s hairstyle doesn't take much effort once your pin-curls are set. Simply make a deep side part above the outer end of one eye and gently brush out any tight curls. Spray, spray, spray in place. You can also use a couple of bobby pins, a barrette, or hair comb to pull hair back off of the face on the sides. That's it!

1948 Joan Crawford bouncy curls

A full head of pin curls using two prong flat clips

Basic 40s hairstyle with one side pinned back. Your hair type and cut will determine how curly your hair will be.

Brush out your hair from the underside and roll the brush at the end so that all curls roll together

1940's Style Guide 51

For a more fashionable and iconic hairdo, you'll have to put in a little bit more effort. Hair was often swept halfway up using pins to hold it in place. The front of the hair had to be tall, made by creating a bouffant at the top of the head. After removing the pin-curls, take a large section of hair at the front of your head, from ear to ear and measuring one to two inches front to back. Hold it straight up and away from your head. On the backside with a fine-tooth comb, start from the middle of the hair and quickly comb to the root, teasing the hair and creating a pillow of hair to support the hairstyle. Once the pillow of hair is big enough, take the front part of hair and fold it over the pillow you've created towards the back of your head. Roll hair under, creating an even, rounded shape, and pin in place. The rest of your hair will still be curly and will be left down. You can also pin up a few more sections of hair behind the bouffant to cover up the ends or pair the bouffant with victory rolls.

Another popular hairstyle at the time was nicknamed the 'victory roll.' This style is a little bit more difficult to master. Once the hair is set, one or more sections of hair are smoothed out and rolled into a circular shape and pinned. There are several ways to do this style, each creating a slightly different look. For a single roll, take a thick section of hair at the front of the head, around where bangs would be if you had them. Smooth the hair back away from your face and roll the ends under, so the hair forms a circular roll shape. Pin the hair in place. Some find it helpful to cheat by rolling the hair with a sponge curler with the plastic portion removed, being sure to cover up the sponge by pulling the hair edges out a bit.

There are two ways to do a double roll. For the first, make the same roll as you did for the single roll excerpt only use hair from one half of your head. For the second roll, take the rest of your hair on the other side and instead of rolling it back, roll it from the side of your head towards the middle. One roll will go from front to back, and the other from side to middle.

Women also wore two side rolls. Part the hair in the middle, and take a thick front section from each side and roll from side to middle. The rolls should be even and sit in the same spot on either side of your head. Hair spray is a must for keeping these rolls in place all day! The rest of your hair can be left in pin-curls, or some sections can be pinned back. Use pomade to smooth out fly-a-ways.

http://www.youtu.be/nfGWqMx81ZM – Victory Roll tutorial for short hair (works for longer hair too)

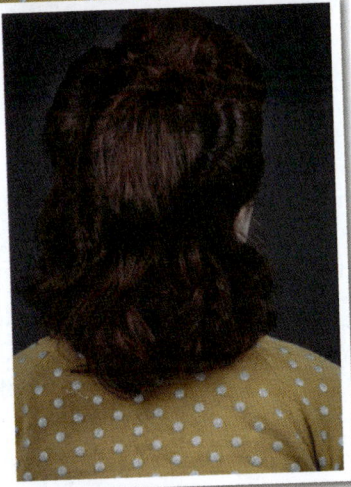

A rolled bouffant created by first teasing the hair to get volume, then rolled and pinned in place

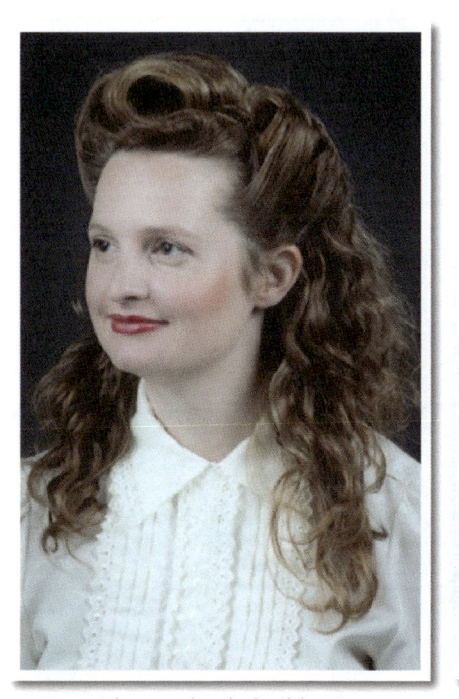

One side, one back double Victory roll

Several Victory rolls gathered from the side

1940's Style Guide

Some other styles took advantage of slightly longer hair and didn't require a full head of pin curls. The "Chinese page boy" can be pulled off with fewer pins. Starting with damp hair, take wads of cotton a couple inches thick and create a long tube with it. Roll the ends of your hair around the cotton tube tightly, towards your head, rolling and pinning up close to ears and the nape of your neck, creating a roll of hair from earlobe to earlobe along the nape of the neck. Tie a ribbon or elastic around your head from your forehead to just above the roll. This will make and indentation in your hair above the curl. After your hair dries, take everything out and tease the bottom layer of your hair, taking care not to mess up the curl. Smooth the top layer over the teased section and pin the sides of your hair behind your ears.

A quick page boy for shoulder length hair doesn't require rolling with cotton. Simply brush under your curls with a round brush and stray in place- a lot of spray. You can also pin your curls to the underside of your hair for more hold.

The 'crescent chignon' was a chic way to pull hair back. To start, set wet hair in the same way as the Chinese page boy 'do above. When hair is dry, take it down and secure it with an elastic. Tease the top of the hair in the ponytail, until it's nice and full and then smooth out the top with a brush. Secure your hair in a bun at the nape of the neck, using an elastic to flip the ends underneath. Now, stick your fingers in either end of the bun (the holes at either side) and slowly pull hair around towards the top until the two ends meet. Pin hair in place.

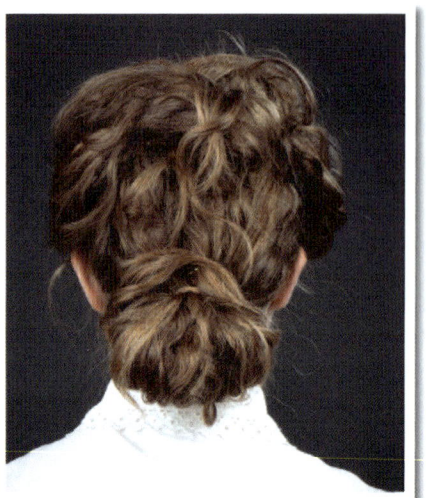

Left: Page boy for shoulder length hair

Colen Gray and Rita Hayworth sporting double Victory rolls

The crescent chignon is a simple tucked in poly tail with wrapped ends, which works best on straight hair

1940's Style Guide

Snoods were a popular hair accessory for both daytime and work. They were rayon or cotton crocheted net or light silk scarves fitted with a headband. The band was worn around the top of the head and all of the hair was encased in the snood. The band was pinned in place. This hairstyle was especially useful for women working in factories because their hair had to be kept back and out of the way. For this style, take the snood and fill it with hair from the bottom. Place the band of the snood where you would a headband and pin in place forming and X with the pins. Pins behind the ears help with hold too.

Hair was also tied up with scarves while working, just like Rosie the Riveter. Take the scarf and fold it half into a triangle. Place the middle of the triangle underneath your hair at the nape of your neck. Tie the two ends at the top of your head with your hair inside the scarf. Take the loose end of the scarf and fasten it inside the tied ends to cover hair completely. Pin in place if needed.

For evening, hair was worn long and wavy or piled on top of the head. The first style was popularized by movies stars like Veronica Lake and Rita Hayworth. Hair was severely parted on one side, past the eye. The thicker side often fell over the eye on that side, and was worn in loose waves instead of curls. The look is fairly simple to do. Part your hair on one side, and take a large curling iron and twist thick sections of hair in spirals. Make sure the curls are loose waves. You can lightly spray your hair for hold, but this look is soft, not severe. The thicker side of hair can be worn so that it drapes over your eye for the full effect.

Tying a scarf, like Rosie the Riveter

Lauren Bacall and Rita Taylor demonstrating long waves both soft and curly

1940's Style Guide

The second evening style was a favorite of movie star Betty Grable. Hair was curled and then pinned on top of the head. To do this style, you can set your hair in pin-curls, but make sure that you roll them tightly and be careful not to brush them out when you take them down. Smooth your hair from the nape of your neck towards the top and do the same on the sides. The bottom and sides of your head should be flat and smooth with no curls. Pull it up almost like you're making a ponytail, but flip the ends up towards your face and pin the curls in place so that all of the curls face forward and are piled on top of your head. Pinning curls underneath the pile of curls keeps hair in place and adds volume to the style. Touch up wild ends with a narrow curling iron, if necessary.

Although very short hair was uncommon in the 1940s a 40s hairstyle can still be achieved. Using either a wet set method or curling iron, curl the ends of your hair in the same direction. Fluff up tight curls to create an allover head of wavy curls. Curling just the hair around the forehead, sides and base of the neck will give the illusion of a fuller hairstyle and were quite popular with military servicewomen who had to fit their hair under hats and helmets. For a more advanced style you can create shapely waves by curling hair in diagonal sections from side to crown or crown to back and then loosely brushing them with a small round brush. The overall look will be geometric and was very common in the early '40s. A quick internet search for how to make marcel waves will help.

http://youtu.be/ro4P_Mou2bs
– War Time Hair Styles video
http://youtu.be/jrMo5wp3q6g
– Creating 40s waves for short hair video tutorial

Betty Grable's iconic 'do with curls piled on top of the head

When styling hair in 1940s styles the most important thing to remember is despite movie star looks and the sheer number of pin up perfect pin curls tutorials on the web, real women in the 1940s spent hours and hours and hours setting their hair. One night's set lasted several days with each successive day becoming less and less perfect. My best advice is to work with your hair. Thin, thick, long or short keep playing with different styles and techniques until you find something that works well for you. I am still experimenting new styles on my very thick, curly, layered hair. It takes time, practice, patience and acceptance that whatever your hair turns out like, is probably what your hair would have been like in the 1940s.

Joan Crawford 1948 hairdo short curls

Hair How To's:

Vintage Hairstyling: Retro Styles with Step-by-Step Techniques – the best book on creating vintage hairstyles using original styling techniques. See:
http://bobbypinblog.blogspot.com/
– for the author's blog with more hair and makeup ideas.
http://retrobelles.com/
– PDF's of original hairstyling books and magzaines
http://www.youtube.com/user/lisafreemontstreet
– Hair tutorial videos from vintage hairstyling books

Hair Accessories:

ttp://www.dancestore.com/
– Basic inexpensive snoods in several color choices
http://www.reddressshoppe.com/
– Carries snoods in every color imaginable
http://www.hairflowers.net/
– Accent your hair with these fun flowers
http://www.cynelena.com/
– High quality hair flowers and clips for pin ups
http://www.littlebellesboutique.com/
– Amazing real looking fabric flower clips, bows, and combs
http://www.flowerclip.com/
– Flower clips, pins and headbands
hhttp://www.mybabyjo.com/
– Rosie the Riveter style hair bandanas

1940's Style Guide 55

Makeup

During the war, European women dealt with huge cosmetics shortages, since key ingredients, like petroleum and alcohol, were used for the war effort. In the United States cosmetics continued to be manufactured throughout the war, and were seen by the government as a morale booster for the busy women on the home front. Women were encouraged to wear makeup all the time to hide sadness and attract men even while at work. Even athletes wore makeup. Color films had a big impact on the market as women could now imitate the shades worn by Hollywood starlets. By 1948, between 80 and 90 percent of women wore lipstick, two-thirds wore rouge and a quarter wore eye makeup regularly. The makeup look of the '40s is classic and sophisticated, but very simple to recreate. Faces were flawless and fresh looking – the look was all-natural, never painted on or heavily made up.

Foundations were not the same as they are today, and not many shades were available, most had a distinct pink hue. They were also much thicker and creamier unlike the lightweight liquid foundations of today. Face powder was an essential, matching the skin tone and keeping the face matte. Foundation was not only used to correct a woman's color and cover flaws, it helped powder to cling to the face, since it couldn't really be used on bare skin without falling off. Foundation and powder was often extended all the way down to the dress or blouse line since the shade most likely didn't match the face perfectly to make it less noticeable.

Blushes, called rouge, were used sparingly and were not available in many shades, and most of those available were pink. Moist cream rouge was used often to give a natural color and was blended into the foundation. Powders were also brushed lightly on the cheekbones to give a rosy look. Rouge isn't completely necessary to the '40s look, and going without it will still achieve the right affect.

Eyebrows were worn fairly natural-looking. Arches were well-groomed, but eyebrows were not plucked to be extremely thin, and only the stray hairs were removed to create a natural arch. They were further defined with eyebrow pencils that were slightly darker than the hair – a line was drawn at the top of the brow and the hairs below were left soft.

Very little makeup was used on the eyes. During the day, most women wore a light coating of dark brown or black mascara, or Vaseline brushed on the lashes. Eye shadows were also worn, but in very neutral colors. Eye shadows matched the eye color, rather than complimented it. Blue-eyed gals wore blue-grey shadow, green eyes used grey shadow and brown shadow was used on hazel, brown or black eyes. For evening, eye shadow colors were sometimes matched to the dress, but often silver or gold was added to a regularly used shade. Eye shadow was worn in a single color (no smoky eyes or contouring here!) from the lash line all the way to the brow and blended. Eyeliner was not used at all.

The lips are the most important part of the '40s face. Lipstick was thought to keep women's spirits up during wartime. Lipstick was red, red and...red! Shades could be bluish or orange-y and everywhere in between, but lipstick was always red and always worn.

Make-up & Beauty

A Vintage 1940's Guide

Bud & Ern Westmore

A Glamourdaze ePublication

1940s Make-Up Guide eBook is 118 pages of original beauty tips and makeup application guides for every type of complexion; highly recommended and available at http://vintagemakeupguide.com/

1940's Style Guide

In the fall, shades became a little darker, and were a little bit lighter in the spring. Steer clear of pinks though, since they were not worn until the '50s. Lipstick was generally completely matte, and women were told not to moisturize lips before applying lipstick to avoid shiny lips. They also blotted lips with a tissue after each lipstick application. By 1948, lipstick pencils had appeared and were being used to perfectly outline the mouth before lipstick was applied. Women tried to plump up their pout using lipstick if their mouth was 'too thin.' They went for an even look – lips should be the same size on top and bottom. If lipstick wasn't available, many women tried natural replacements like beet juice with Vaseline over the top.

Although this all sounds very simple, a woman's makeup routine in the '40s could take a while – the five minute face did not exist! First, the thick foundation had to be applied and blended. Women were encouraged to shape their face with lighter and darker shades of foundation. Darker shades could be used to 'fix' a large nose, big forehead, or square jaw. A lighter shade on cheeks could make them look plumper. Next, they applied the eye shadow, and after that, moist rouge was applied. This could also be used to shape the face, but had to look natural. Then powder was applied with a huge velour or wool puff. It had to be pressed into the face and was applied heavily before the excess was brushed off the face with a powder brush. If the moist rouge was not enough, a powdered one was applied over the face powder. Finally, women applied the eyebrow pencil, mascara and lipstick.

Fingernails were always neatly trimmed and filed into oval shapes. Nails were kept slightly shorter during wartime work for safety. Cuticles were also always kept immaculate, trimmed and moisturized. Nails were almost always painted in various shades of red, although pink, mauve, rose and burgundy were also popular colors. One fingernail fad was to leave the half-moon white spot at the base unpainted – this was a classic fingernail style of the 1940s.

Today it won't take much makeup to finish off your '40s look. Just paint your nails red, put on plenty of face powder and black mascara, define those brows, put on a flattering shade of red lipstick and you're good to go!

For more tutorials, I would normally suggest turning to website on 1940s makeup. However, in my opinion, there are few quality sources. Most online videos and tutorials lean on the modern or pin-up side of makeup instead of the natural 40s look. Use them as a suggestion, but stick to the style explained here and you will be glamorous in no time.
http://www.youtube.com/

watch?v=75TwRLgxMXo
-1940s Fashion Film on how to apply makeup
http://www.besamecosmetics.com/
-Nice vintage color choices in beautiful cosmetic cases

Tip:
An easy way to create an even half-moon shape on your nails is to use stick-on hole paper reinforcements. Apply the labels to the base of your nails. If the top of the inside hole is just touching your cuticles, then the polish lines will be right where you want them. Apply polish. Remove labels after one minute, but before completely dried. Apply clear coat to finish.

Tip:
Purchasing modern makeup to create a 1940s look is not easy. Most modern colors are shiny, glittery, bright and otherwise unsuitable for the natural '40s look. You will want to find makeup that is pure matte without any shine. Revlon makes a good matte line, as do some of the newer organic makeup lines. Max Factor and Elizabeth Arden were original 1940s brands, and thus still have a few colors in their modern line. Besame is another line that recreates vintage makeup colors and cosmetic cases. My personal favorite pure Red lipstick is L'Oreal Infallible Le Rouge Lipstick #308.

Men's Fashion History

Men's clothing in the 1940s, either for day, sport, or evening was styled to make a man feel larger than life. During the years between 1941 and 1945, WWII fabric rations limited cloth to make suits but not the style of the suit. The Zoot Suit with its bright colors, baggy legs and long jackets was a complete deviation from the traditional suit. However, that trend was only popular with the young men during the war years. Most men chose basic men's suits that haven't changed dramatically since the beginning of the century. There were, however, a few features that make a suit style unique to the 1940s.

The war board placed restrictions on men's clothing just as they did women's, but the restrictions were not as dramatic as they were for women. Suit pockets could not have flaps, trousers could not be more the 19 inches around or be cuffed, and suits were sold without vests (waistcoats.) The cuffed look was so popular that men quickly figured out you could purchase longer length pants and cuff them at home. Double breasted suits were forbidden during the war except for formal occasions, such as weddings. Most men kept their clothing from the 1930s and wore their older suits through the early '40s war years. Tailors became skilled at repairing or repurposing double breasted suit jackets from the 1930s into single breasted jackets or sport coats. It was a sign of support for the war to be seen in your pre-war suits.

In Britain the clothing restrictions were harsher. Jackets could not have pleated backs, metal zippers or buttons, feature raglan sleeves or have half belts. Zippers in flies, called front fly fasteners, were allowed although button flies were preferred and easier to obtain.

War time clothing influenced men's fashion design after the war by copying or modifying uniforms into civilian clothes. Trench coats, bomber jackets, knit undershirts, pea coats, chino pants and aviator glasses all have their roots in WWII-era military clothing. With so much military surplus available after the war, civilians bought and wore military clothing for several more years. The improvement in machinery, textiles and manufacturing of military clothing made post war ready-to-wear civilian clothing a booming industry. The quality and eventually affordability of ready-made clothing gradually put local tailors and seamstresses out of business.

The biggest influence war time restrictions had on men was an increase in casual attire. After the war, suits were often replaced by more causal sporting attire. Collarless knit tee shirts, open collar dress shirts, ascot ties, slip on loafers and sandals in summer became the everyday man's dress code. Men were tired of scratchy uniforms and confining suits. The freedom of casual wear was a relief.

Ironically, the very clothing that caused such turmoil during the war years, the Zoot Suit, was the single piece of fashion that influenced men's post war clothing the most. Longer, looser jackets, double pleated pants, big hats, and even wider ties made their way into late 40s men's fashions. Men were eager to put the war behind them and embrace the clothing they were previously forbidden to wear.

A gentleman in a pinstripe suit and polka dot tie

Men's Clothing

The Suits

Regardless of an increase in sportswear, during the '40s, suits were still every day wear for men, whether they were going to an office job, to a picnic, or out to dinner. They were also probably the most worn piece of a man's wardrobe. They were usually made from wool, worsted wool, or tweed, but during the war synthetic rayon blended with wool was usually used instead. The thickness of suit fabrics was much heavier than today's suits, and colors were muted. Black, navy, grey, dark brown, tan and medium blue were all standard. During the summer, fabric was more lightweight as were the colors.

The most popular colors for summer during the '40s were a medium grey, brown, medium blue and tan in the warmer months. Tweed, herringbone, check, and plaids were popular suiting patterns. Wide chalk stripes were also a classic '40s suit pattern, and pinstripes became popular later in the decade. Almost every suit had stripes or a pattern to it. For a more casual look, a plaid jacket was mixed with plain pants, or vice versa. Another trend in plaids was a jacket that had plaid sleeves and a solid body or plaid body with solid sleeves worn with coordinating trousers.

The suit jacket was single-breasted and although square, much slimmer than its '30s counterpart. It had two to three buttons that were less than an inch in diameter since button size was restricted. Shoulders were padded and the jacket tapered into the waist. The lapels were wide notch or peak with rounded edges. Jackets usually had two front slit pockets since patch pockets used too much fabric, although they came back even bigger after the war. Jackets were worn with a hint of shirt cuff peeking out from the sleeves.

Before the war and occasionally after, men wore a matching vest or waistcoat with their suits. They were considered a wasteful item in war time and after, most men preferred not wearing a vest with their suits at all. It was cooler and more comfortable without them. Besides matching the suit, vests were V neck cut with pockets on either side, one of which could hold the watch and chain that commonly dangled from the vest.

Clark Gable and Tilly Shelton-Smith

Double breasted striped suit
Wearitagainvintage (etsy.com)

1947 casual men's wear

1940's Style Guide

The suit trousers were usually flat-fronted, but they could have single pleats. They were worn at the high waist with a three-inch waist band. Belt loops were placed in the center of the waistband so that the belt sat centered about an inch down below the top edge of the waistband. Trouser legs could be no more than 19 inches wide around the ankle, quite wide by today's standards. Usually they were straight hemmed at the bottom as required during the war; however, men preferred having two-inch trouser cuffs (turnups), so they purchased pants longer then they needed and cuffed them at home to get around the law. In France, a 1 ¾-inch strip of material was allowed to make a faux cuff, but it was so small it was hardly noticeable. Trousers were worn long enough to cover the tops of shoes, but not so long that they bagged up at the bottom.

After the war, soldiers in Britain were given 'demob' (demobilization) suits to wear. They were very plain and of poor quality, usually made in a late '30s style, but at least they were not a uniform. After rationing ended, double-breasted jackets with wider lapels came back in style and were worn more frequently during the '50s. The influence of this wide, loose, bold suit came from the forbidden Zoot Suit.

Single and double breasted sport coats

Dress trousers in plaid, stripe, and solid wools

Single breasted summer weight suits; note the large patch pockets on the suit on the left

Casual Trousers

Trousers sold separately for casual day wear, sporting events, and some work environments were a bit more colorful and more comfortable then suit trousers. They were made of lighter weight wool blends in the cooler months and even lighter cotton poplins, gabardine (rayon blend) or seersuckers for tropical climates. Solid colors of green, blue and tan were staples, while more unique patterns like plaid, pinstripes, diagonal stripes, pin check and herringbone in medium blues, maroons and browns were favored. They featured a narrow, high waist and full hips with straight wide legs. Flat fronts were preferred over pleats, but both were acceptable and available. Waistbands had dropped belt loops, and were worn with a thin leather belt. Shirts were worn tucked in, and rarely matched the pants. Instead tan pants were matching with maroon shirts, plaid with brown, or pinstripes with blue.

Sports coats too were a newer trend that gained popularity in the 1930s. These came in a smattering of glen plaids, herringbone, chevron checks, chalk stripes and tweeds. They were worn with solid color pants that were darker than the sport coats, with the exception of white pants which were always worn with a navy blue sport coat.

Sport coat materials were a bit heavier then suiting materials, with wool blends being the most common. They were lined in silk before the war and rayon after the war began. Sport coats had wide rounded notch lapels, two very large pockets and 3 button closures. Pockets came in a variety of flap, slit or patch styles, and angled pockets were popular with slit and flap varieties. A chest pocket was always included to hold a colorful pocket square, for decoration rather than use.

Two-tone sport coats

Tweed sport coats were especially common in Britain

Casual trousers worn with matching collared shirt or knit T shirt

Casual trousers

1940's Style Guide 61

1940's Style Guide

Collared Shirts

The collared dress shirt was a must-have item for men during the '40s. These shirts were usually made from cotton with an attached, large and pointed collar. Collars were soft with removable collar stays for structure. They pointed down a tad and outward toward the shoulder. Shirt lengths were short by today's standards, but could be tucked in and were almost always worn that way. Shirt backs and arms after the war had pleating to allow extra room for movement.

For work, a long-sleeved collared shirt was worn under the suit jacket. Work shirts were made of mercerized cotton or rayon blends for some shine and came in white, blue or tan, sometimes with stripes or a subtle art deco print. They might have no pockets or, especially after the war, a single patch pocket on the chest.

Casual collared shirts could have long or short boxy sleeves and were straight cut at the bottom. They could be worn untucked, but tucked in was preferred. Large soft collars were worn closed, just like dress shirts, but more often were worn open with the top button undone. Shirts came with two chest pockets, in welt, button, or fold over flap styles. Colors could be plain tan, brown, blue, green or maroon, and plaids, checks, windowpane, and stripes were very popular for casual wear.

The Hawaiian Aloha shirt was brought back from the war featuring hand painted tropical scenes, birds and flowers. These were worn un-tucked and fit rather loosely. These became especially popular throughout the 1950s. Western shirts and trousers were another trend that started in the mid-40s and grew even more popular in the 1950s. Hollywood's wave of American western movies spawned an interest in western style clothing for both boys and men. Western shirts, hats, boots and trousers were equally popular with city and country folk. You could say that the urban cowboy began in the 1940s.

Western shirt pattern
Sovintagepatterns.com

Dress shirt pattern
Sovintagepatterns.com

1940s Hawaiian shirt featuring girls, palm trees, and Hawaiian words
SweetMoonlightShop (etsy.com)

Casual plaid shirts

Dress shirt with subtle art deco print

Knit Shirts

A casual lifestyle opened the flood gates of for men's knit shirts, vest and pullovers. They felt nothing like todays' smooth jersey knit t- shirts. These were made of textured ribbed knits, often hand knit at home, but mass produced as well. They fit very snugly with a wide rib bottom and smaller ribbed sleeve and neck bands. Necks were almost always round and high on the neck, or a small V-neck. They could be worn tucked in or un-tucked, but were usually tucked into the pants. They came in a wide range of textures and colors. Solid colors, wide horizontal stripes, and "Norwegian" designs for winter were especially common.

Knit V-neck vests or pullovers were made in the same style and colors as shirts, but were worn over a long sleeve dress or casual shirt. In winter, they were knit of wool for extra warmth, and in summer they were made with rayon/cotton blends. This three piece look was especially popular with golfers and sport spectators. Pullovers usually contrasted with the shirts underneath and with the trousers creating a very colorful outfit. For example, a tan shirt with green slacks and a blue pullover, or a wine colored shirt with navy pants and a grey pullover might be worn. The combinations were endless, making knit vests and pullovers popular, since the mixing and matching allowed for a smaller wardrobe to be purchased.

A stylish 40s knit pullover vest

Knit "T" shirts were very popular with young men

Knit shirt pullovers

Sweaters

The sweater was a classic casual look during the '40s, carrying into the 1950s, and worn with casual slacks just like the pullover vest. They were worn fairly fitted, especially during the war due to wool shortages, and came to just below the pant waist with a wide ribbed band. Colors were not widely varied – dark brown, charcoal, navy, hunter green and maroon were the standards, but they could also be found in red, yellow, blue, cream and lighter grey for spring fashions. Stripes and Fair Isle patterns were most popular in winter along with the "Norwegian" designs.

Some pullover sweaters had a wide or cabled ribbing with a wider ribbed hem and cuffs, in a crewneck or a small v-neck style. Cardigans were a very popular look, with a v-neck and buttons down the front or a zipper and small stand-up collar. Cardigans often had two low front patch pockets as well. For extra winter warmth, cardigans sometimes had a large shawl collar that could be worn down or up could be wrapped with a warm scarf.

Button up knit cardigan sweater

Winter pullover V neck sweaters in plain and "Norwegian" designs

The Zoot Suit

The Zoot Suit was a style of dress that became popular during the late 1930s among young people, particularly young African Americans and Mexican Americans, who were into swing dancing and jazz music. The suit itself was loud and extremely loose, and reached the height of its popularity in the early and mid '40s. When wartime rationing restricted the amount of fabric that could be used in men's suits along with everything else, the Zoot Suit technically became illegal. The means to get enough fabric to make the suits required purchases made on the black market or from underground tailors. Young people continued to wear the style despite the restrictions, and the suits soon became associated with delinquency and crime. Most wearers were simply rebellious youths, many in inner city urban areas like Harlem and Los Angeles, who were trying to form a culture all their own. The wearers of Zoot Suits were seen as being unpatriotic, and tensions between Zoot-Suiters and military servicemen stationed in California erupted in a week of violent street fighting in Los Angeles in mid-1943 that came to be known as the Zoot Suit Riots.

The man's Zoot Suit consisted of an extremely long and wide two-button suit jacket, with large notch lapels, and huge shoulder pads, worn over extremely baggy trousers that came well above the waist reaching almost halfway up the chest. The pants tapered at the bottom to a very tight cuff at the ankles and were held up with suspenders. A plaid button-down shirt, tie, shiny leather shoes and a wide-brimmed fedora hat completed the look on the east coast. On the west coast, the tie and hat were replaced by hair greased back into a tail. The Zoot Suit was usually wool, often in black pinstripes, plaids or very bright colors like red, royal blue, yellow and purple. Some Zoot Suit styles featured a dark suit jacket worn over light Zoot "chino" pants. Homemade jackets had very large patch pockets on either side. Extra wide and short ties, matching pocket square and big fluffy bow ties were most popular with performing

Tension between street kids and military men erupted in the week long Zoot Suit Riots

I want a Zoot Suit
with a reet pleat
And a drape shape,
and a stuff cuff
To look sharp enough
to see my Sunday gal

"A ZOOT SUIT"
(For My Sunday Gal)
L. Wolfe Gilbert /
Bob O'Brien

1940's Style Guide

Around the world other rebellious youths adopted the Zoot Suit look. In France the Zazous wore oversize suits with short trousers exposing bright white socks and platform shoes. A wild print tie, thin mustache, quaffed hair and a rolled umbrella finished the look. In Germany the "Swing Kids" danced in underground parties to the new American jazz music. They wore double breasted pin stripe suits with high pinched in waists, extra-large lapels and carried a rolled umbrella. To achieve the oversized suit look many economical young men purchased suits in a few sizes up and modified them to form the tight waist and shorter trousers.

It is interesting to note that despite the Zoot style being considered unpatriotic during the war, afterwards the style became the new men's look of the late 40s and early 50s. Large double breasted baggy suits with high waists, pleated trousers and wide brim hats returned to fashion, just as they were in the 1930s, but now with a taste of the Zoot in them as well.

http://www.suavecito.com
– Off the rack or custom made men's Zoot Suits to tent or buy
http://www.elpachuco.com
– Reproduction Zoot Suits, shirts, shoes, hats, and accessories

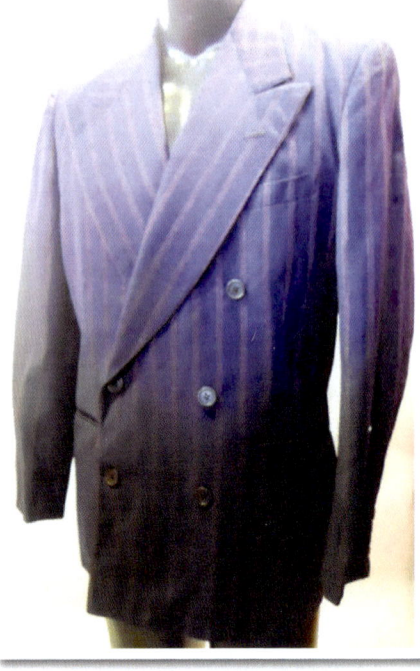

Zoot suit trousers

A late 40s doubled breasted chalk stripe suit inspired by the Zoot suit

Formal Wear

During the war, for various reasons, dinner jackets were rarely worn in public places....and this custom has taken root in America, particularly among the younger generation .
-*Vogue's Book of Etiquette* (1948)

In the new era of simple taste formal clothing became the extreme exception rather than the norm. Tail coats and double breasted dinner suits were banned during war time and never regained their required status. Only very formal occasions such as weddings, classy restaurants, formal balls, and opera performances encouraged formal dress, but could not enforce it for the sake of the poorer younger generation. Besides tail coats, formal bib front dress shirts were replaced by a quality white button up pleated dress shirt. Wingtip collars were ousted in favor of soft fold over pointed collars. Patent leather shoes were replaced by shinny calfskin shoes and satin replaced braid as the stripes on formal pants.

Formal peak lapel dinner jacket, wingtip white shirt, black bow tie. Lady in mesh top two piece gown with white opera length gloves

The dinner jacket (cousin of the tuxedo coat) and matching vest (waistcoat) was considered semi-formal enough for most formal occasions. Midnight blue was favored instead of black because it looked better and showed less dirt in artificial light. A solid color necktie and matching pocket square in colors of black, midnight blue and maroon completed the semi-formal look. While single breasted dinner jackets were the norm during the war, the double breasted jacket style took over after restrictions were lifted. For most men, however, formality ended by choosing to wear their best suit to any after six event including their own wedding.

The only exception was a return to summer formality with white single or double breasted shawl collar dinner jackets worn over dark trousers. This look started in the 1930s with regular sightings of movie stars on cruise ships heading to tropical climates. After the war, men were eager to return to this popular look.

Double Breasted shawl collar dinner jacket and single breasted peak lapel jacket.

Military and Work Wear

Where did all that wool go during the '40s? Well, it was needed to clothe the brave men and women in the military. Since there were so many different variations of uniform and factions of the military I will just touch on the basics here.

The standard issue army uniform consisted of sturdy wool slacks and a wool button down shirt in 'olive drab.' Cut like regular clothing, the shirt had two large patch pockets on the chest that buttoned at the top and was worn tucked in with a thick leather utility belt. The slacks were tucked into mid-calf leather lace-up boots, and an olive wool garrison cap or metal helmet completed the uniform.

The standard working U.S. Navy uniform worn aboard ship was a matching shirt and slacks somewhat similar to the U.S. Army uniform, except they were made with indigo denim. The shirt was a button up, but instead of a pointed collar it had a small shawl collar and the oversized patch pockets were on the bottom of the shirt instead of on the chest. The slacks also had large pockets on the sides. Leather boots and a white 'Dixie Cup' hat finished it off. The "Navy Blues" were for formal wear.

Air Force officers wore a similar uniform as well in the same color and shape as the army uniform. However, they wore a thin olive tie with their shirts and did not tuck their pants into their boots. Their uniforms were topped off with an aviator cap and a brown leather flight jacket.

Navy uniforms

1940's Style Guide

Outside of the war and after, men still had a work uniform. For those who did not wear suits to work a collared shirt and work trousers in sturdy cotton twill or gabardine was traditional. Work trousers had flat fronts with a single leg crease. The leg widths were narrower than suit or sport pants, and colors were fairly basic tan, brown, navy, and hunter green, although occasionally plaid was chosen. A matching trouser and shirt set was common for most lines of work. Work shirts had open soft pointed collars, two patch pockets, and pleating at the back and arm holes for freedom of movement. A solid color tie worn with the work outfit kept men looking appropriate in public settings.

Sturdy cotton canvas coveralls were worn by men that had to get dirty on the job. These were all one piece, and buttoned down through the fly with straight legs. They belted at the waist, had long sleeves for protection and had a pointed collar. They also had big patch pockets on the chest for keeping things handy. Overalls were worn over a work shirt and came in plaid or dark denim blue, as well as industry specific stripes like those worn by railroad men. Farmers favored overalls for the loose, comfortable fit and ability to add or remove layers throughout the day.

Military uniform worn as civilian clothing

Military dress uniforms

Swimwear

Briefs were the trend for the beach or pool, but these were not the tiny Speedos of today! Fabric technology certainly was not where it is today, and many were simply rib-knit wool. However, rayon 'Lastex' fabric, which utilized spandex for stretch and dried much faster than wool was coming into use, eventually replacing wool and cotton altogether. The briefs of the 1940s were cut very high in the waist and had low-cut legs. Colors were usually dark like navy, hunter green, blue, and maroon. Some had little patch or zippered pockets on the front and a thin fabric belt.

Swim trunks were becoming more popular during the '40s. The shorts were made with cotton and had an elastic waist. They were worn with a high waist and were cut straight coming to mid-thigh. Trunks were usually in the same colors as briefs, but were also available in loud tropical prints. They were worn with a matching short-sleeved button-up shirt.

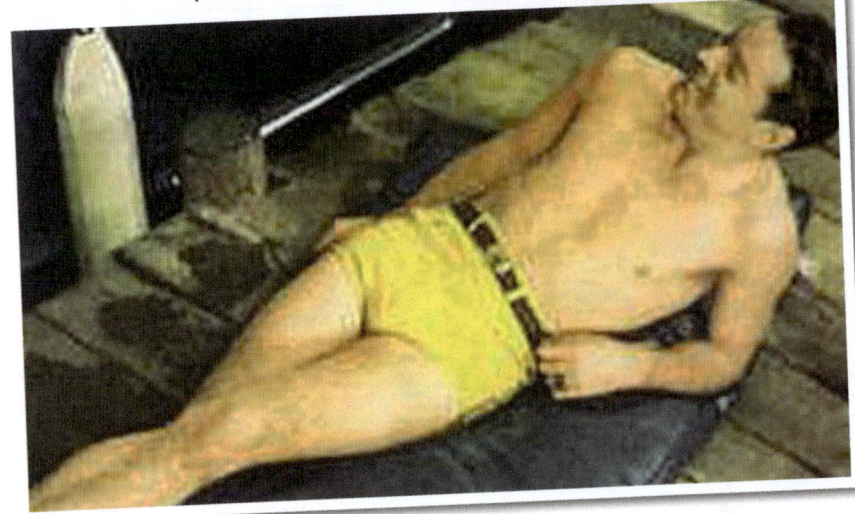

1947 yellow swim shorts with belt

Sleepwear

During the '40s, men didn't just throw on an old T-shirt and boxer shorts to get into bed. They had to look presentable too! Matching cotton pajama sets were always worn. They consisted of straight-leg pants with a high elastic or tie waist and a button down shirt. The shirt might have a pointed collar, but could also be a crew or v-neck. Long, white nightshirts were still worn by men during the '40s. The top was the same style as the regular pajama shirts and fell straight to the knees. Checks, stripes, paisley prints and plaids added some flair to PJs.

1940's Style Guide

Just like '40s women, men always threw a robe on over their pajamas to lounge around the house. Men's robes had padded shoulders, came down to the knee or mid-calf and were worn wrapped around and tied with a belt. They usually had a large contrasting shawl collar. Made from cotton flannel, gabardine, terry cloth and rayon, they came in colorful plaids, stripes and loud patterns. Jewel tone satins of blue, maroon, green or wine were the most handsome choices. A waist length robe, called a smoking jacket, was worn over day clothes at home to protect them from smoke and ash damage.

Slippers were another essential item for the '40s man. They looked like loafers, with penny, oxford or plain tops of brown or tan leather and a soft, warm fleece lining. The "opera" cut slipper was the most unique with a V notch cut out on the sides (slipper on the far right.)

Underwear

Men's underwear, unlike women's, has not changed much throughout the years, although it did look a little bit different during the '40s. Men wore either briefs or shorts. White briefs were made from ribbed cotton with an elasticized waist and were worn high on the waist. Shorts were woven cotton and were either white, blue or had a small print on them. They buttoned or snapped in the fly and had either elastic panels on the sides or a drawstring tie waist. They fell to the upper thigh.

Men always wore an undershirt during the '40s. Before the war, a white ribbed cotton scoop-neck tank top was the standard undershirt but with thinner straps than men's undershirts today. However, the white cotton T-shirt was the standard issue undershirt for soldiers, and it soared in popularity during the decade. That's even how it got its name – it was called the 'T-type shirt' by the military. After the war, the T-shirt as a clothing item came to be – men started wearing them by themselves without anything over them as they had become accustomed to while overseas.

During a cold winter, men might throw on a "union suit" underneath their clothes. This was simply long underwear. The '40s version was fitted with buttons down the front. The legs reached down to the ankles with long or short-sleeves. The "union suits" were usually white ribbed cotton with a crew neck. Short leg varieties with short or tank top sleeves style were an alternative to just undershorts in spring or autumn weather.

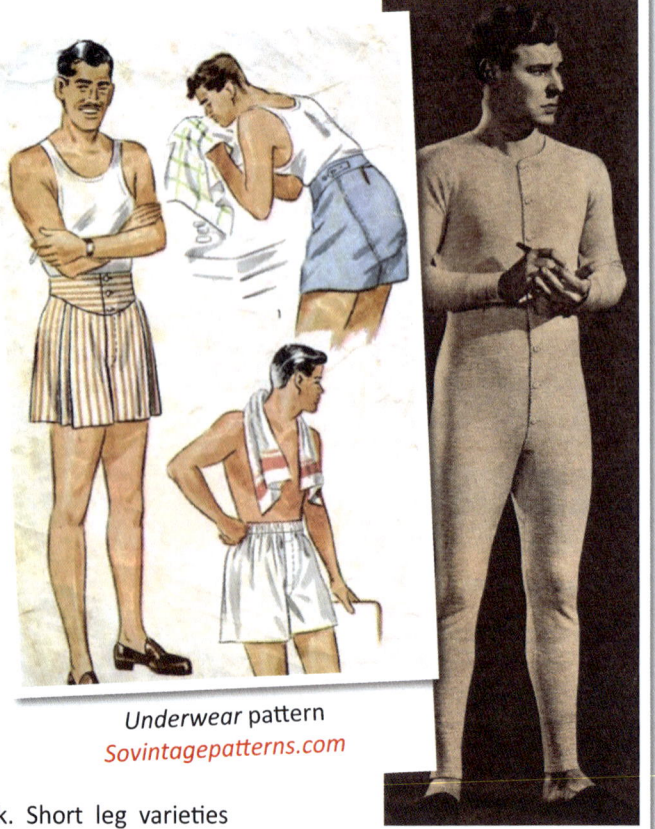

Underwear pattern
Sovintagepatterns.com

Union suit

Outerwear

A wool overcoat was a winter staple for the '40s man. The overcoat was cut straight and very boxy, coming down to the knee at a very slight angle. The shoulders were rounded and sometimes raglan cut. They had very wide, peaked lapels and side angled slit pockets. The buttons down the front were covered with a long flap. After the war, when wool restrictions were lifted, a double-breasted version became popular. It was worn with a wide belt at the waist. These overcoats were usually tan, plaid, tweed or herringbone with a plaid cotton flannel or rayon cotton blend linings.

The trench coat was another classic '40s look, made popular by Humphrey Bogart in the 1942 film Casablanca. It was the same shape as the overcoat – boxy and to the knee. It was originally worn without a belt and had side slit pockets and a very small pointed collar with virtually no lapels. Later in the decade a double-breasted version with a wide belt came into fashion, like Bogart's trench in Casablanca. This version had epaulets on the shoulders, wrist straps to keep the dampness out and a D ring belt loop that originally was used for carrying grenades. Trenches were cotton gabardine, almost always in tan.

Air force flight jackets were one of the most sought after military items for civilian wear. They were made from brown leather and sometimes had a cream fleece lining. One version came to the waist and had a pointed collar. Thick cotton ribbing at the cuffs and hem kept it snug. Another version was a little bit longer and belted at the waist with big front patch pockets or two. De-regulated flight jackets were quickly snatched up by teenagers in the post war years.

Simple winter wool overcoat

Military bomber jackets were slightly modified and sold to civilians

Humphrey Bogart in Casablanca made the trench coat famous

1940's Style Guide

Flight jackets made of wool, instead of leather, became known as the Eisenhower jacket. Commissioned by Dwight D. Eisenhower as the "Wool Field Jacket M-1944," Eisenhower wore it often to meet troops in the field. It was short, fitting snugly at the waist, with wide sleeves that cuffed tight at the wrists. Since Eisenhower was widely photographed in the media wearing his jacket, it took on a star status on the home front. Young boys who grew up watching their heroes go off to battle were eager to wear the Eisenhower jacket after the war, especially if it was given to them by a male relative or close friend.

For spring and fall, a lighter jacket would do. Made from wool or cotton poplin they had buttons down the front, pointed collars, and small lapels. Patch pockets held the essentials. Some jackets were a pullover style without buttons. They had cotton ribbed cuffs and hems instead. These had crew or v-necks. Colors were kept neutral – tan, brown or navy. For a spiffier look, navy or hunter green panels were inset into the fronts of tan jackets.

One of the most icon and collectable '40s jackets today is often called the gabardine jacket, after the material. It was made of a rayon and cotton twill blend that had a soft shine to it. The smooth material was crafted into a very plain jacket with angled slit pockets on the sides, five buttons down the front or zipper in the later '40s, and an optional chest pocket with a flap. The jacket hung straight down to the waist and was fitted only with a half belt at the back and two adjustable side belts. The jacket collar was soft, with wide points worn loose and open for the most casual comfort. They came in military colors, like tan, olive green, navy and grey.

The Eisenhower military jacket. Civilian jackets were made of cotton twill

A poplin cotton waterproof pullover jacket

Gabardine jacket in tan

Double breasted overcoat

Men's Accessories

Hats

During the '40s every man had a hat on his head! The fedora, also called a trilby, was by far the most widely worn style. Fedoras of the 1940s had a 2½-inch to three-inch brim and a tall pinched front crown with a center crease that was either flat-topped or angled to the back. Made in wool felt, they were grey, black, dark brown, tan or cream. The brim was bound in petersham ribbon in the same color as the hat. A one-inch to two-inch wide matching petersham ribbon hatband added some flair. Later in the 40s, a black or striped hat band added to any color hat was trendy. A flat bow on the side, with or without small feathers, added even more interest. For a more casual day, men wore fedoras made of cotton twill or straw. How men wore the fedora was a matter of personal taste. New hats came unshaped so that the customer could direct the hatter to shape it according to his preference. Many wore it with the brim flat all around and angled down slightly in the back; others with the back angled up, and some with the brim turned down in back and up in front and on the sides. Movie stars often started a trend for one brim shape over the other. They also influenced whether the fedora was placed straight on the head or angled to the right side, the latter being popular with Hollywood gangsters and detectives.

In tropical climates, wool hats were too hot. Instead, woven straw hats in the shape of fedoras, porkpies and boaters were worn as they had been for the prior two decades. Simple straw hats with wide brims that angled down and rounded crowns were the working man's straw hat. The shape is similar to a soft bucket hat today. Middle and upper class men's straw hats usually had colorful hat bands wrapped around the crown. Bright solid colors, horizontal stripes and patterns like polka dots were all common. Clashing color combinations like pink and blue or sport's team colors added personality to your look.

New black felt fedora with flat grosgrain bow and feather

Summer cotton bucket hat

Pinch front fedora hats with front down and back up brims

"Safari" summer hat

1940's Style Guide

During the summer, men often wore sun helmets when they were enjoying the outdoors. They were tan cotton twill, and looked like safari hunting hats. Metal eyelet vents provided extra cooling in warm weather. Baseball caps were also worn, but the brims were much shorter and rounder than are found today.

The other popular felt hat of the 1940s was the homburg. It came only in grey or blue, along with black in the early '40s. Black faded out of fashion by the mid-'40s. The crown was quite tall with a moderate center crease. The brim was curled all around but especially on the sides creating an oblong-shaped fit. The curled edges were less tight than they were in the previous few decades creating a wider, looser, fitting hat. Black petersham ribbon bound the brim and hat band. The trend was to wear the Homburg slightly pulled forward and down on the forehead. This was the last decade for the Homburg's popularity, other than a short surge of trendiness in the 80s, when The Godfather movies were released.

The most unusual hat of the 1940s was the porkpie hat. Similar to a Victorian gambler hat it came in black or brown fur felt and featured a short oval flat top with deep crease around the oval. A wide curled brim all around with matching petershambrim makes the porkpie stand apart from the gambler. Worn at an angle with a thin leather hat band or a wide petersham ribbon with a flat bow in the same color as the hat, the porkpie hat shared some qualities with other felt hats of the 1940s.

During the war young boys and older men swapped their traditional hats for military hats to show their support for the troops. The abundance of military surplus hats after the war kept military hats in style for most of the early 1950s.

Porkpie hat with feather and bow trim

Top to bottom: Straw fedora, boater, bucket, homburg, porkpie

1942 homburg hat

http://www.vintagedancer.com/1940s/1940s-mens-hats/
- New 1940s style hats

Shoes

The go-to shoe for the '40s man was the leather lace-up oxford in mellow brown or matte black. These oxfords were thinner than today's, with rounded toes. Dressier styles had a slightly pointier toe, but square toes became more popular during the late '40s and into the 1950s. Oxfords had a small stacked heel and leather sole. After the war, soles began to be made from rubber. Colors were tan, brown or black, although white was available during the summer. Oxfords were often decorated with intricate patterns made with holes punched into the leather called brogue, in wingtip designs for more formal wear or across the vamp or cap of the toe for casual looks. The most formal shoes were made of shiny patent leather rather than traditional matte leather.

Perhaps the most iconic shoe of the 1940s was the two-tone oxford. Black and white or brown and white oxfords came in many patterns. Toe and heels could be dark with the light color in the middle, or the tops white and bottoms dark, or white shapes could be laid over a dark base. Two-tone shoes had been popular since the 1920s, but what makes the 1940s unique is the lack of intricacy in the design. The two-toned shoes came in blocks of color, rather than the elaborate swirls and patterns of the previous decades. By the 1950s, two-tone saddle shoes with white toes and heel and a dark middle became the trademark shoe for both young men and women; however, saddle shoes were equally common in the 1940s.

A gentlemen looking fine in his two toned oxfords

Black and white leather wingtip shoes

Vintage two tone brogue wingtips made of canvas and leather

1940's Style Guide

Because leather was in such short supply for civilians, men's shoes were very expensive to purchase. A single pair of leather oxfords could use up half your ration stamps for an entire year. Unlike women, men were not fond of shoes made from reptile skins or synthetic materials. The only non-leather shoes they accepted and wore were fabric oxfords made of cotton canvas weave in either brown or grey. Some varieties had low wedge soles and one hole per side for laces. They were not rationed and were not very expensive but they did not last long. Wood soles were also tried to reduce the cost of men's shoes. These could not withstand the elements very well, nor were they comfortable at all. Most leather oxfords were fashioned with rubber soles that were easy for a cobbler to re-sole. This made shoes last longer and well worth the additional expense. A single pair of well-made leather oxfords with soles replaced yearly could last the duration of the war.

Fabric shoes were worn more often in summer because they breathe better than solid leather. Basket weave leather oxfords were another summer favorite. The woven leather design was used for the sides, vamp and other portions of the shoe. This allowed cool air to filter through and provide some relief in tropical climates. Basket weave shoes were available in American moccasin styles too. Moccasins were slip on shoes with or without two eyelets for laces, a strap and buckle to the outside, or penny loafer styles. The toes could be smooth or outlined in crimped leather, and inside they were lined in comfortable wool felt fabrics for winter or cotton for summer. Moccasins were much more casual than any men's shoes had been before, but it was perfectly acceptable to wear moccasins with your sporting attire, and possibly even with a business suit for lower class positions. Topsider shoes were popular with young men. These were moccasins with a lace that wove all around the shoes and a bow tied on the tongue, associated with the sport of boating in the 1930s. Topsider shoes were also called deck or boat shoes.

Kangaroo leather work boots and shoes

Purchasing fabric shoes did not require a rationing stamp

Freeman shoes- (from left to right) Saddle, two tone oxford, two toned brogue wingtips, basket weave oxford, two toned oxford

Perforated oxford and moccasin shoes

1940's Style Guide

For hard working jobs, such as farming, railroading, and mechanics, men wore sturdy work boots. With thick heavy rubber soles and high leather bodies that rose above the ankle to provide support and stability for long days, work boots laced up part way and hook and looped the rest. Various grades of leather determined the quality of work boots, and their intended purpose. Elk hide was the softest and appropriate for light, indoor work. Tanned cowhide was tougher with a coating of rubbed oil to make them waterproof, and was better suited for the outdoors. Kangaroo leather imported from Australia was advertised as 17 percent stronger than cowhide, and these were some of the top of the line work boots a man could buy.

During the summer, men wore leather sandals with their casual outfits. In tan or brown, they had crisscrossed wide leather straps over the top of the foot, a very small opening at the toe, and an ankle strap with a metal buckle. The idea of men wearing sandals was still a bit foreign to many men, so it took most of the 1940s to gain the popularity that they had in the 1950s.

Sports shoes were coming into their own as an option for leisure took, even though today we can not imagine not having several pairs of comfy sneakers. The '40s versions resembled Keds or Converse with cotton or leather uppers and thick 1-inch rubber soles. In fact, classic All Star Converse sneakers were invented in 1917 and have been mostly unchanged in design since then. White Converse high tops were official men's training shoes during the war and were equally popular with Olympic athletes. They came in both low and high top versions in navy, brown or white with white laces. The classic black and white combination didn't come about till the '50s. .

Sandals with cut outs and T strap

Sport shoes in high and low tops

Socks

Socks were worn fairly tall, to about mid-calf. Work socks came in shorter, above the ankle, length. They were made of ribbed wool, cotton or rayon blend with tighter ribbing on the top inch or two to hold them up. They were dark colors like brown, tan and blue, or light white and grey. Just like ties socks also came in a wild range of colorful stripes, art deco patterns, and argyle designs.

Because the socks were not elastic, they tended to sag. Sock garters helped to hold them up. These were an elastic or leather strap with two clips that grabbed the sock and another clip that wrapped around the calf tightly and held the garter in place.

Top: Ribbed, argyle, deco pattern socks
Bottom: Argyle, striped, solid color socks

1940's Style Guide

Belts

Suspenders were not really worn by men in the '40s, unless they were older men or were part of the Zoot Suit underground fashion movement. Belts had largely replaced suspenders as pants became more fitted at the waist. They were about an inch or so wide with small metal buckles that were often covered in matching leather. The leather was tan, brown or black and could be plain, pebbled, braided or even stamped with a Western motif.

Watches

Now that everyone carries their cell phones with built-in clocks around with them, watches are falling by the wayside. During the '40s, the wristwatch was a requirement for men. Watches sometimes had circular faces, but a square or rectangular face was much more stylish. They had thin gold trim around the face, and a brown, black or tan leather band. The band was much thinner than watches of today, measuring around ½-inch wide. Watch bands were smooth leather or pebbled.

Cufflinks

Cufflinks were almost always worn with dress shirts, especially for work or fancier occasions. They were usually gold-toned metal with pops of color done in glass or resin. Geometric art deco designs were a trend during the decade as were monogrammed initials. Nautical themes were big too – an anchor or boat would be surrounded by navy. Plain circles or squares were filled with colored glass. Other cufflinks had themes like lucky horseshoes, planes, palm trees or pin up girls. Since they were worn so often, men collected many different pairs.

Gold cufflinks set in blue resin and white anchors
WaxwingJewelry (etsy.com)

Pocket Squares

No 1940s suit would be complete without a pocket square otherwise called a handkerchief. These were made from rayon or silk after the war and were often brightly colored or had paisley or other classic patterns. They were folded and placed in the chest pocket for looks. These were not used for practical purposes – that one stayed in a pocket and was made of white cotton.

Scarfs

While a knit wool scarf provided plenty of warmth in colder climates the most common use for a scarf in the 1940s was as a fashion accessory. Pilots in wartime wore a white silk scarf while at home men wore bright patterns of paisley, stripes and deco prints. Scarves were worn hung around the neck, crossed in front and tucked into the jacket or pullover vest. In many cases, a scarf was worn in place of a tie.

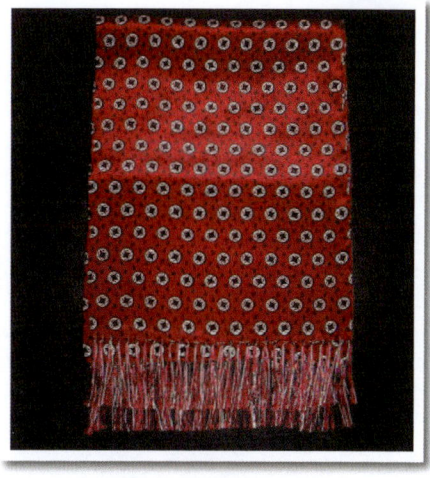

Men's vintage scarf
NeatClassics (etsy.com)

Ties

No suit would be complete without the perfect tie! Ties were made exclusively from silk until the war hit, and were made from rayon and wool until it was over, when silk made a comeback. They were panel ties (made from one piece of fabric) and fairly wide, tapering a bit towards the top and were Windsor knotted. They were short, coming to about two inches above the pant waist.

During the '40s and into the '50s, wild ties were a huge fad. Men amassed huge collections of them and tie-swaps and tie-swapping clubs were popular. At the time, ties were a way for men to show their individuality and optimism after the uniforms and hardships of the war.

Crazy and loud patterns were in style. Geometric curly line monograms and a deco style pattern were made in bright colors. Animals, plants, flowers, birds, Western and tropical themes were everywhere. Ties were often themed around the wearer's hobbies and interests, like painting, fishing or hunting. The crazier the tie, the better! The most expensive and sought after were hand-painted silk tie although most men wo mass manufactured tie The panel style tie allowe multiple ties to be cut fro the same piece of cloth, wit the pattern silkscreened o printed onto the same spo along the length of it

Wide '40s tie with art deco design

1940's Style Guide

One American trend was the "Belly Warmer" tie, with a hula girl and palm trees painted on it. Introduced as a joke, the belly warmer ties became trendy after actors like Bob Hope, Alan Ladd and Danny Kay were seen wearing them. Soon after, scantily clad pin-up girls painted on the back side of a tie became fashionable in public.

Although less popular than neckties, bowties were still an option for neckwear. Solid colors, as well as prints like paisley, made the bow tie a handsome accessory. Mostly worn by men from older generations, the bowtie continued to lose favor in the 1950s, especially in the USA.

In Britain, the ascot tie was even more popular than the necktie. An ascot is a large rectangular piece of silk or rayon that is loosely wrapped around the neck, simply knotted and tucked into the pullover, sweater, or jacket. The most common color was white, although gray and other solid colors were welcome too. The ascot provided warmth and casual, comfortable fashion to the British.

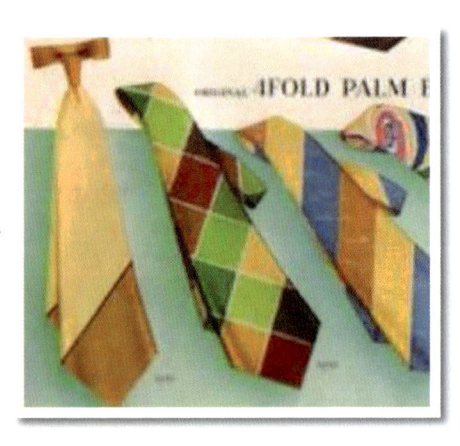

Hairstyles

The 1940s man had perfectly groomed hair, with frequent visits to the barber. The look is fairly simple to pull off today (unlike those time-consuming women's styles!) First, the perfect haircut is a must. The cut was short on the sides and back, and longer on the top. That length is needed to complete the 'do!

It is very important to the '40s hairstyle to have shiny, wet looking hair that stays perfectly in place. During the '40s, this was achieved with one of a few key products that are still available today, even though most men now would not touch them. By far the most widely used hair product was Brylcreem, hair cream in a tube! Murray's pomade is another good choice and is much thicker for more serious hold. Both of these products will make your hair greasy. While that's the goal, make sure to give it a good wash if you opt for these authentic choices! Two other products were used a lot by men in the '40s, but they do not work as well for the desired look. They do give hair a ton of shine, but not a lot of hold. Wildroot Cream Oil has a medium consistency and Vitalis Hair Tonic is more like a liquid.

Now that you have your haircut and styling product of choice, all you need to complete your hairstyle is a comb. Start off by loading your hair up with the styling cream or liquid of your choice, and combing it through thoroughly. Make a very straight and defined part on one side of your head. The part should be right where the longer top section of hair meets the closer-cut side section. Next, starting at your hairline in front, comb hair up and to the side, making a little side-swoop on top. Comb the rest of your hair so that it's slicked back making sure that it looks even across the entire top of your head. That's it – the perfect '40s hair!

Advice for Dressing as a 1940s Man

Luckily for men, putting together a 1940s style outfit is not nearly as difficult as it is for women. Unfortunately, men's vintage clothing is much harder to find and often not in very contemporary men's sizes. Local thrift stores and antique shops are a great resource for finding suits and shirts while online shops can complete your outfit for harder to find accessories. Here are some tips on what to look for:

The suit should be either single or double breasted, but you will look more stereotypical of the 1940s in a double breasted striped suit. Very wide lapels in either notched or peaked cut are a must! Lapel widths have come in and out of fashion for the past 60 years, so it is quite possible to find these locally. You may even be able to find one new at your local department store. Suits described as classic cut typically have medium width lapels, a loose fit and wider trousers than slim fit suits. Be sure to buy cuffed trousers or cuff extra-long trousers yourself.

For a sport coat, the ones from the 1970s work very well. They are often made in vibrant patterns with wider lapels. The tricky part is resisting the urge to buy those funky orange and yellow '70s coats. Choose plain, checked and muted solid colors for a more accurate '40s look. Pair your sport coat with a pullover V-neck sweater vest and you are halfway there.

1940s wide-leg trousers can be harder to find in thrift stores. Specialty sport stores with a golf section will provide you with traditional golf slacks with double pleats and wider cuffed legs. The main challenge with new trousers is that they are designed to fit below the belly button, rather than just under the rib cage, like they were in the 1940s. One solution is to purchase a pair of trousers one or two sizes up, so you can pull them up higher on your waist, and use a thin leather belt or suspenders to hold them in place. If you are handy with a needle and thread, you can even move the belt loops down an inch for more accuracy.

A comfortable swing dance outfit: pin stripe pants, wingtip dance shoes, button down shirt, wide tie, suspenders and fedora hat

Oscar wearing a shawl collar tuxedo, french cuff white shirt, black bow tie, and fedora hat. Debbie is wearing a red wiggle dress by Stop Starring Clothing and a fur trim black shawl

1940's Style Guide

Just like sport coats, 1970s dress shirts will give you the widest pointed collars at the thrift store. Modern western shirts usually have double pockets and sometimes have pointed collars which make them good choices as well for a casual '40s style. Most contemporary dress shirts have short collars which will look wrong when worn as a sport coat alone, but could be fine if you also wear a pullover vest, tie and sport coat.

A 40s hat is a must have accessory for your outfit. Avoid modern narrow brimmed fedora hats. While they will do just fine in a pinch, for a little bit more get an original wide brim style fedora, and really impress your friends. Vintage hats are quite expensive so you may want to go online for more affordable reproduction hats.

Wear your best brown or black dress shoes. Standard men's shoes are still in the same lace up oxford style as the '40s. Do not wear sneakers. Go the extra mile and splurge on a nice pair of two-toned oxfords if you dress up regularly. If you swing dance, then invest in a good pair of two-toned dance shoes.

Be clean shaven. 1940s men did not have facial hair. The look is in the details. For a classy event, be sure to add cufflinks, a pocket square, watch on a chain, and slicked hair. The additional effort will really make you look the part.

A '90s double breasted three piece suit, two tone wingtip shoes, fedora hat and tie

Men's Shopping

Here are a few vintage and vintage inspired 1940s clothing retailers for men:

http://www.rustyzipper.com/
– A very diverse collection of vintage 1940s men's clothing
http://www.sazzvintage.com/
– Men's vintage from Rockabilly to Disco
http://www.vintagedesignerclothing.com/hawaiianshirts.html
– Many hard to find top designer vintage clothing. Great Hawaiian shirts for men
http://www.jabotsboutique.com/
– A decent collection of men's vintage clothing. 1940s items sell fast
http://www.ballyhoovintage.com/
– A good mix of vintage clothing
http://www.revivalvintage.co.uk/
– (UK) A small mix of 1940s vintage clothing
http://www.savvyrow.co.uk/
– British vintage clothing auction site. Top quality!
http://www.tweedmansvintage.co.uk/
– Vintage suits, clothing, and accessories
http://www.revampvintage.com/
– Reproduction clothing for swing dancers
http://www.somelikeitholy.com/
-Men's reproduction trousers and vests
http://puttin-on-the-ritz.net/men/
– A few reproduction 1940s suits, trousers, and vests
http://www.juke-jive.de
– (DE) Probably the best online site for reproduction clothing
http://www.wwiimpressions.com/
– Reproduction WW2 Military Uniforms
http://www.paulfredrick.com/
– Modern clothing with a fine classic style
http://www.jpeterman.com
– An ever changing line of men's clothing that often includes vintage style tweed jackets, shirts and pants in the 40s style
http://www.josbank.com/
– Excellent provider of new classic menswear, especially formal suits and casual golf pants.
http://www.hats.com/ or http://www.villagehatshop.com
– Both carry new fedora, homburg, porkpie and straw hats.
http://www.dancestore.com/ or http://www.swinggear.co.uk/
– Carries two tone dance shoes in vintage styles
http://www.evadress.com/
– Men's vintage reproduction patterns
http://thefedoralounge.com/
– The place to go online to ask a question with other vintage stylish men
http://www.gentlemansgazette.com/
– Excellent blog about men's suits through the decades
http://www.pomade-shop.eu/
-Pomade and mens grooming supplies

Making a 1940s Outfit
Sewing with Vintage Patterns

Despite the many great vintage and reproduction clothing options available on the market, you may have the need or desire to make your own clothes. Picking a pattern, fabric and trim is an exciting process. Luckily, we have several options for custom-made clothes that match our sewing skill level, or lack thereof. Our first and most difficult option to create a 1940s dress or suit is sewing an outfit from an original 1940s pattern for men or women. There are a few reason why using a vintage pattern is challenging.

Pattern sizing has changed over the last 60 years. To put it nicely, clothing manufacturers have altered their sizing to provide lower numbers than they once did. Pattern companies stuck to true sizes in the 1940s. While pattern sizing has changed less than fashion sizing, it has changed somewhat since the 1960s and 1970s. On the right is a vintage '40s to modern size comparison for women.

This is a general guide. Each pattern maker has different measurements for different sizing. Be sure to read the measurements on the package, and keep in mind waist measurements are your high waist, at the narrowest point, rather than your low waist, near the hipline.

Each pattern comes in one size (not multi sizing like today) so there is no wiggle room on the pattern for adjustment. You can, however, buy any size pattern and enlarge or shrink it to fit your size. There are many books on the market that teach you to resize patterns. I would suggest you acquire one of these, particularly one focused primarily on sewing vintage patterns. Often, even if you buy your correct vintage size pattern, you will want to make some adjustments to the patterns. Vintage clothing fits differently especially in the arms. Arm holes were smaller and higher up into the arm pit, restricting movement. Bodices also had a tighter fit to keep you standing straight and sitting properly. Making adjustments in these areas will certainly increase comfort, but they may also alter the overall look of the garment to the point that it loses its '40s styling. Decide what activity you will be using the outfit for and adjust accordingly. Swing dancers will need more arm movement than those wearing '40s attire to a party.

Besides the differences in fit, sewing with a vintage pattern has other challenges. Patterns were not written with the same markings as they are today, and may not give you notches to match up fabric pieces, or tell you how pieces should be cut, or what the "right" and "wrong" sides are. A good book on how to read vintage patterns will help you out if you do opt to sew with vintage patterns.

If I have managed to scare you away from sewing clothing from vintage patterns, please do not be. There is something really amazing about using original patterns, but they do take more time and care. Do not be afraid, just take the time to learn the language first and always make a cheap mock up with muslin before cutting or sewing with the good fabric.

1940s Pattern Sizes vs. Modern Size

12 -------- 4
14 -------- 6
16 -------- 8
18 -------- 10
20 -------- 12
40 -------- 14
42 -------- 16
44 -------- 18

Advice:
http://www.blogforbettersewing.com/2010/06/vintage-pattern-sizing.html
— How to resize a vintage pattern as well as an excellent blog to follow
http://wearinghistoryblog.com/
— Another excellent blog on sewing with vintage patterns
http://www.sovintagepatterns.com/resizing_vintage_patterns.html
— Resizing vintage patterns guide

Vintage Patterns:
http://www.sovintagepatterns.com/
— A huge collection of patterns for all types of clothing
http://www.lanetzliving.net/
— Vintage and vintage modern, retro, and new patterns
http://www.momspatterns.com/
— Great out of print patterns sorted by decade
http://www.vintagestitching.com/
— Affordable vintage patterns
http://www.oldpatterns.com/
— Organized by type and decade

1940's Style Guide

http://www.sew-retro.com/
– A nice collection or vintage patterns

http://www.vpll.org/
– Reprinted vintage patterns to borrow or buy. Amazing!

Reproduction Patterns

If you feel that your sewing skills are not advanced enough for a vintage pattern, you can use a reproduction pattern. Reproduction patterns are based on vintage patterns, but have been altered for modern bodies, and marked with modern pattern construction techniques. You will find these are much easier to work with, yet they still create a beautiful garment with all the style and flair of an original '40s dress.

There are a handful of reproduction pattern makers, and each one has their own level of difficulty. I recommend doing an online search for a review of a pattern before buying. Patternreview.com is an excellent source for both reviews and online sewing lessons.

http://www.pastpatterns.com/1940.html
– Reproduction patterns you'll love

http://www.agelesspatterns.com/
Reproduction dress patterns

www.decadesofstyle.com/
– Patterns for aprons, dresses, blouses, skirts, playsuits and pants

http://www.reconstructinghistory.com/
– Reproduction patterns to fit modern bodies and sewing techniques; men's patterns too

www.longago.com/forties.html
– Some unique 40s reproduction patterns

http://www.wearinghistorypatterns.com/
– A few dress, hat and playsuit patterns from the 1940s

http://www.edelweisspatterns.com/patterns.php
– 1940s dressed based on the Sound of Music movie costumes

http://www.thetailorsapprentice.com/ (Dress pictured on the Left)
– (AU) 1940s dresses, overalls, wedding gowns and online classes to learn vintage sewing techniques

http://www.evadress.com/40s-01.html
– Dress, slips, skirts, blouses, and trousers. Men's trousers, jackets, ties, and smoking jacket

http://www.neheleniapatterns.com/
– (DE) German pattern maker of women's historical and vintage clothing

http://rockinghorse-farm.com
– Small collection of 40's clothing patterns

Fabrics:

Here are some sites that sell Vintage Fabrics. Remember most fabrics in the 40s were Rayon, cotton or wool blends.

http://www.rickrack.com/
– Original fabrics from the 1940s- mostly cotton prints.

http://www.antiquefabric.com/
– Large collection of original fabrics

http://www.vintagefabrics.com.au/
(AU) Many colorful fabrics for home and clothing. Ships worldwide

http://www.vintagefabricmarket.co.uk/
– (UK) Vintage fabrics, accessories and some vintage clothing

http://www.donnaflower.com/ (UK) Charming collection of 1940s fabrics

Notions:

http://www.thebuttonbower.com/
– Buttons, buttons, buttons

http://www.accessoriesofold.com/
– Beads, buttons, trim, and more

http://www.dressingvintage.com/
– Button cards and loose button, clothing, books, patterns

http://www.vintagebuttons.net/
– Buttons, jewelry and more

Modifying Modern Patterns

One of my favorite, quick and easy ways to make a 1940s style dress is to modify a modern dress pattern into one with a 1940s style. When I first tried this I was nervous, since had never strayed from a pattern before, and I was afraid I wouldn't know what to do. Depending on your level of sewing skill, you can get very creative with your modifications, or keep it simple. Here is how I kept it simple using Simplicity 2615 as an example:

1. Start with a picture of a dress from the 40s that you like. I find it easier to consult a vintage 40s dress pattern rather than a

photo from the 40s.

2. Notice the overall shape of the dress. Is it an A-line? A wrap dress? Is the skirt pleated or gathered? Are the sleeves long, short, or capped? Next look for a modern pattern that shares the same silhouette and sleeve shape. Some current dress patterns you might consider are Simplicity 1882 and 2247, New Look 609, 6587, and 6674, and Burda 8510.

3. Adjust your pattern where needed. If your pattern has a round neck, but you need a square one, just trim away the excess. Sleeves can be lengthened, shortened or shaped. Add pockets, belts, and buttons for more vintage details. For my dress shown to the right, I used Simplicity 2615 and reshaped the sleeves to curve, reshaped the neck into a sweetheart cut instead of round neckline, and added a belt.

4. Choose a vintage looking fabric and coordinating trims.

5. Accessorize your final outfit with vintage jewelry, hat, purse and shoes.

Vogue 1940s day dress pattern and my dress inspired by the pattern

Hire a Seamstress

Your last option to get custom-fit 40s clothing is to hire someone or ask a giving friend or family member to make one for you. This is an ideal option if you can not sew, do not have the time, or have a size that is not easily found in vintage clothes or modern reproductions. Because it does take considerable time to make custom clothing, you will find pricing for a simple dress starts around $100, without material cost. Choosing inexpensive cotton will reduce your cost, but will also reduce the overall quality of the garment. If you are going the custom made route, I suggest you be prepared financially to make it worth it.

http://www.etsy.com/shop/nudeedudee
– An Esty seller who makes custom '30s, '40s and '50s dresses
http://www.etsy.com/shop/

MissCherryPieRetro
– A designer and dancer specializing in 1940s tea length dresses
http://www.etsy.com/people/jacksdaughter
– Custom dresses, blouses, and playsuits in colorful fabrics
http://www.etsy.com/people/VeconaVintage
– (DE) Men's and Women's custom trousers, vests and dresses
http://www.corinacorina.com/
– (UK) Carries vintage clothes for sale, or hire and a few dress, skirts and sweaters for custom made orders
http://www.swingoutfits.com/
– Many dress, skirts, blouses, pants for Women and trousers, shirts and bests for men. Ideal for swing dancers of the '30s and '40s
http://www.customclothes.co.uk/
– (UK) Made to order '40s, '50s women's and men's clothing. Great styles and fabrics

One final word about custom made clothing. You need to remember that custom made clothing is handmade clothing. You will not find factory-finished perfection in any garment. Depending upon the skill of the seamstress and the machinery used, it is perfectly acceptable to find different seam finishes, hand-sewn details and even a few loose threads. If you were to look inside handmade vintage clothes from the past, you might be horrified to see the quality of sewing in what looks like a perfect garment. The final result is all about the outside, never the inside. Just remember this when or ordering custom work and you will not be disappointed.

Shopping

Where to Shop

Vintage clothing and reproduction clothing have different qualities and price ranges. As with most things in life, you get what you pay for. Buying cheap will not mean high-quality, but for a one-time event, it can be a perfect choice. However, there are other ways to get great quality outfits at amazing prices. Here are some tips:

Thrift or Charity shops: These are my favorite places to shop. Most real vintage pieces are sold to high-end vintage thrift stores and personal collectors, but that does not mean a 1940s style outfit can not be pieced together. For example find an A-line skirt and match it with a white blouse or sweater. Wrap dresses and shirt waist dresses have been popular for years and can be really easy to find. Look for men's overalls for a Rosie the Riveter look.

Garage Sales or Estate Sales: Can be a gold mine for vintage clothes. They can also be time consuming, so most people only choose to go this route if they are dedicated collectors or enjoy the hunt.

Friends and Family- You will be amazed at what is hidden in your neighbor's closet. Use email or social sites to send out your request for vintage clothing. Most will be happy to let you at least borrow an outfit for a special night.

Costume Rentals: Not the cheapest option, but if you can find the main outfit at a thrift store, then consider renting hat, shoes, fur coat or other high end accessories. This will be cheaper than buying these items outright. I generally suggest you stay away from cheap party costumes. The styles are neither historically accurate nor comfortable, and are made of cheap, non-breathable polyester. Some costume accessories may work for short-term wear.

Antique Stores: Prices run the full gamut on clothing, but I find many antique collectors simply do not know much about clothing. Often, I can find great deals on hats, gloves, shawls, jewelry and shoes, simply because the seller does not know what they have. They also mislabel clothes with the wrong decade so be sure to look at everything, regardless of what the tag says.

Department Stores: Wherever you normally shop for modern clothing you will probably find many 1940s inspired styles. You probably never noticed them before, but now that you know what a 1940s style outfit looks like you will spy them across the room and go running in a mad dash before anyone else has a chance to claim your vintage find. Okay, so that probably does not happen to anyone else but me. Nonetheless, vintage and retro 1940s fashion is in style now. You can find a great outfit anywhere you shop. If you do not see the clothing you want right away, try looking in a different section of the department store. For example, if you wear juniors' sizes, you probably never go into the 'mature' women's sections of the store. Well, now is your perfect opportunity. The older the target clientele, the more likely you are to find 1940s-style clothes. The same can be true the other way, since retro styles are in vogue with teens and young women, mature women should check out the teen section, particularly for accessories and shoes.

What to look for

When shopping for 1940s clothing, many new buyers will end up picking out a 1980s dress believing it is genuine '40s. The style, the colors, the padded shoulders, and sometimes even the materials can fool you. The 1980s revived interest in 1940s clothing just as the 1970s revived 1920s clothing and the 1990s revived 1930s. Vintage fashions are always making a comeback in some form or another. Currently we are seeing a 1920s revival.

1980's? 1940's?

The one great thing about fashions of the 1980s repeating the 1940s is that we have plenty of affordable choices to help us create the look of the '40s. Some of my favorite dresses are '80s does '40s. Wrap dresses, shirtwaists, ruched garments, and pencil cuts are all popular '80s and '40s styles. Most of the time, no-one knows that I am wearing an '80s dress, especially when it is accessorized with vintage '40s jewelry and hat. Wearing '80s clothing is a great way to start your '40s wardrobe quickly, and it is easier on your budget too.

Some things to consider when buying 1980s does 1940s clothing:

Shoulder pads are not the same. The 1980s shoulder pads were huge round, and thick, while '40s shoulder pads were narrow, long and square. I suggest cutting out '80s shoulder pads and replacing them with '40s pads or removing them all together. A great tutorial on making vintage shoulder pads can be found here:
http://blog.caseybrowndesigns.com/2010/07/vintage-sewing-techniques-shoulder-pads

Prints in the 1980s got a little crazy, as did the colors; pink, bright blues, and shocking yellows. Some '80s dresses, despite having the right shape and style, do not have the right colors. Choose 1980s dresses in the '40s palate of navy, green, brown, and creams.

Fabrics in '80s dresses are almost all polyester (yuck!) They do not breathe well, but despite that, they look and feel like '40s rayon. Polyester dresses are fine for low-key wear, but I do not recommend them for vigorous activities like dancing. 1980s cotton dresses, like shirt dresses, are a much more comfortable choice.

An '80s peplum dress- very '40s

An '80s velvet black dress is timeless, add vintage jewelry for a '40s look

An '80s pleated dress in a wonderful 40s style print

A houndstooth coat dress doubles as a '40s style dress or coat

A '90's pink coat looks very '40s with the big buttons and pockets

1940's Style Guide

Shopping Online

A lot of what I have said about shopping on a budget locally can be said for shopping online. Here are a few more tips worth repeating:

1. In most cases you get what you pay for. Pictures lie, so you should always read descriptions. Avoid any fabric with greater than 50% polyester. Even 100% cotton fabric can have night and day differences- look at the price to determine its quality. The cheaper the price, the more likely you will get a stiffer, rougher fabric that feels more like craft or quilting cotton, than soft fashion cotton. Rayon is your best friend and the most authentic 1940s fabric.

2. Know your measurements and shop by these, not by modern sizing and certainly not by general small, medium and large tags. Even modern clothing suppliers should have a sizing chart on their website. Look at these before choosing your size, and call customer support before buying if you are unsure.

3. Vintage clothing retailers usually do not label clothing by decade properly, if at all. Shopping portals like eBay and Etsy are great for finding vintage, but do not trust their labels. Quality vintage retailers usually only resell high end items with the price tags to match. Everyone else labels their items with their best guess or no guess at all. You can find cheap 1940s clothing items by looking for clothing that's only labeled "vintage" or "retro" or just "old." The less descriptive the title, the less likely the seller knows what they have, and the more likely you are to find a diamond in the rough. Other sellers use every potential label imaginable on a garment, so that it's most likely to turn up in search results. Again, don't trust their labels entirely. Use the information in this book to help you pick the real 1940s clothing out from the rest.

4. No matter how big an online shop appears to be, often just one to three staff run it. Be nice, be understanding, and be patient with these mom and pop stores. The customer service will be great, but shipping and processing could be slow. If you have a deadline, be sure to talk with them first so they can meet it. Also, plan ahead if you are shopping around holidays. Some small stores close early, even weeks early, around holidays and during popular vintage conventions.

Show and Tell

Fabulous men and women are dressing up in 1940s clothing with vintage, reproduction, 1980s, vintage inspired or a combination of it all.

Charly Surry in 1980's green leaf viscose dress teamed with a pale high neck jumper, a cropped herringbone brown jacket, two- tone modern brogues and a vintage brooch.
www.landgirl1980.co.uk

1940's Style Guide | 89

Caitlin Farthing wearing a vintage Victory suit and repro Aris Allen dance shoes

Stephanie Wolff dressed as Rosie the Riveter

Lauren Reeser wearing a handmade 40's dress from a vintage pattern
americanduchess.blogspot.com

Lori Crandal Wearing a Vintage '40s Dress

Audra Kleiner wearing vintage In front of a 1940s Dodge

Resources

Vintage Clothing Suppliers

Here are many of the best, or at least my favorite, vintage clothing online retailers that have a decent collection of 1940s clothing. Most carry dresses, skirts, blouses and other garments, and some carry harder to find shoes, coats, hats, bags and jewelry. Check them out and be sure to visit often as new items are added daily.

http://www.snap-it-upvintageclothing.com/
– A good collection of vintage finds
http://www.1860-1960.com/
– One hundred years of fashion & accessories
http://portervintage.co.uk/
– (UK) A new addition to the vintage clothing world, with over 400 pieces. Mainly sourced from the UK, and some pieces purchased from the well-known Kerry Taylor Auction house
http://www.ballyhoovintage.com/
– Men's and women's clothing, aprons, hats and more. Nicely organized site
http://shop.circavintageclothing.com.au/
– (AU) Love this large site for quality garments
http://www.vintagetrends.com/
– Both women's and men's clothing. Great selection of coats and blouses for women and Military Uniforms for men
http://www.tangerineboutique.com/
– Vintage clothing, accessories, and sewing notions
http://www.hollyvoguevintage.com/
– Jabot's is devoted to bringing you the finest quality authentic vintage fashions on the Internet; they carry dresses (conveniently sorted by size), coats, loungewear and accessories
http://www.poshgirlvintage.com/
– One of the more popular vintage clothing sites. Easy to navigate. Items sell quickly
http://pastperfectvintage.com/
– Amazing quality clothing from the Victorian era on up
http://www.vintagetextile.com/
– A very high end, amazing quality, vintage collectors site
http://wearitagainsamvintage.com/
– Another nice shop of 1940s vintage pieces. Men's too
http://www.wallflowervintage.com/
– One of my favorite vintage stores

Vintage reproduction Cloting

These stores feature authentic vintage designs made new with modern sizing and tailoring to fit bodies without girdles.

http://www.revampvintage.com/
– Probably the best quality vintage reproduction clothing. Limited edition production means your item remains as rare as the vintage pieces that inspired the look
http://www.reddressshoppe.com/
– Another large collection of vintage inspired dresses, coats and hair snoods!
http://www.vivienofholloway.com/
– (UK) Nice reproduction trousers, tea dresses, blouses, and skirts
http://www.tarastarlet.com/
– (UK) The best for last. This designer includes many more 1940s clothing styles in her collection than other designers

Vintage Modern Clothing

New clothes with elements of 1940s styling, let you join the latest fashion craze where vintage meets modern!

http://www.vintagedancer.com/1940s/1940s-womens-clothes/
– My mix of 1940s inspired dresses from all over the web.
Plus sizes at :
http://www.vintagedancer.com/1940s/1940s-plus-size-dresses/

http://www.revival-retro.com/
– (UK) A very nice site of dresses and shoes for the 1930s and 1940s swing dancers
http://www.bettiepageclothing.com/
– A line of retro vintage dresses, skirts, and blouses. Very cute designs
http://www.whirlingturban.com/
– Retro-modern pin up style clothing and wedding gowns
http://www.heydayonline.co.uk/
– (UK) A few cute 1940s dresses
http://www.20thcenturyfoxy.com/
– Classy styles with many options for the plus sized gal
http://www.stopstaringclothing.com/
– My favorite for '40s and '50s cocktail dress styles
http://www.mybabyjo.com/
– A mix of '40s and mostly '50s style clothing, swimsuits, shoes, jewelry and accessories
http://www.unique-vintage.com/
– A mix of vintage modern brands all in one site
http://chicstar.com/
– An affordable favorite for 1940s inspired pin up dresses in a wide range of sizes

Shopping Portals

http://www.ebay.com
– Still a popular auction and shopping portal for vintage items.
http://www.rubylane.com/
– A vintage marketplace
http://www.etsy.com/
– Probably the best portal for vintage and handmade clothing online.

Stay Connected - Blogs, Magazines, Social Sites

Although there are only a few online and offline resources about the 1940s, the ones that exist are quite helpful. Stay connected with other 1940s fashion fans at these sites:

http://www.1940s-fashions.co.uk/
– One of the best blogs on 1940s (and other era's) of fashion. She also finds original videos from the 1940s that feature how to tutorials, fashion shows, and TV advertisements
http://1940s.org/
– A tribute to the1940s and film noir. Blog posts about history, fashion, music, radio and movies of the 1940s
http://vintagebulletin.blogspot.com/
– Vintage retailers' blog. Many different vintage clothing collectors post information about their latest items for sale
http://www.retroradar.com/
– News for those who love a retro vintage lifestyle in modern times. Also the maker of the very popular forum:
http://www.thefedoralounge.com/
– Ask questions and get answers on all your 1940s fashion needs
http://www.diamonddame.com/
– Fashion, lifestyle & music of the 1920s, 1930s and 1940s
http://glamourdaze.com/
– Wonderful blog and videos from several vintage decades
http://www.landgirl1980.co.uk/
– Dressing 1940s with 1980s clothing
http://fortiesknitter.blogspot.com/
– Knit with 1940s patterns
http://fortieswardrobe.blogspot.com/
– How one woman designed a 1944 wardrobe over five years. Fascinating in depth look at the 1940s.

Recourses
More on and offline help for learning about 1940s history and fashion.

Books
Baker, Patricia. Fashions of a Decade: The 1940s. 1992, Facts on File, Inc.

Baxter-Wright, Emma. Vintage Fashion: Collecting and Wearing Designer Classics. 2007, Harper Collins Books

Mendes, Valerie and Amy De la Haye. 20th Century Fashion. 1999, Thames & Hudson

Olian, JoAnne. Everyday Fashions of the Forties As Pictured in Sears Catalogs. 1992, Dover Publications, Inc.

Walford, Jonathan. Forties Fashion: From Siren Suits to the New Look. 2008, Thames & Hudson

Worsley, Harriet. Decades of Fashion. 2007, Tandem Verlag GmbH

Website
http://www.centuryinshoes.com/decades/1940/1940.html
– A brief illustrated history of 1940s shoes
http://www.headoverheelshistory.com/1940.html
– A Research project turned history lesson on shoes
http://www.1940s-fashions.co.uk/ – (UK) A very nice collection of fashion plates and advertisements featuring fashion from the 1940s

www.thepeoplehistory.com/40sclothes.html
– An interesting look at fashion and how much clothing really cost
www.womeninwwii.com
– A site all about women who served during WW2 in the 1940s

Images
http://www.shorpy.com/
– A collection of public domain and member contributed vintage pictures
http://memory.loc.gov/ammem/index.html
– Library of Congress collection of photographs
http://www.flickr.com/commons
– A mix of public domain images
http://pinterest.com/source/1940s.org/
– One of many 1940s fashion pages collected on Pinterest

Contact Me

Congratulations, you have made it to the end of the 1940s style guide. Assuming you read every word you are now an expert on 1940s fashion! Okay, maybe not an expert, but certainly much more knowledgeable than before.
If you have a questions about anything I have not covered in this book-please email me. My personal email is Debbie@vintagedancer.com I check it often and will be more than happy to answer your questions.
Thank you again for purchasing his book. I hope you enjoyed reading it as much as I enjoyed writing it.

About the Author

Fashion history should not be ...well history. Bringing fashion back to life is an amazing journey of understanding the culture and society in which the clothing was worn paired with the who, what, and where details of the garments themselves: Who wore this? What did it look and feel like? Where would it have been worn? These are the questions that drive Debbie to research and write about fashion history you can wear.

Creator of VintageDancer.com, a vintage inspired clothing aggregate website, Debbie Sessions helps shoppers dress in vintage style clothing, shoes and accessories from Victorian to the 1960's. Along with her husband, Oscar, they have years of experience dressing in all eras of clothing. And they dance too! (Mostly swing, Victorian couple dances, contra, and a bit of salsa.) Together they live in Reno, Nevada, USA with their daughter, Autumn, two cats, and a vintage 1920's house to call home.

More books in the style guide series are coming soon.

Acknowledgements

Thank you to Lisa, Lauren, Maryke and Michelle for your help and expertise in advising, writing, editing and designing the 1940's Style Guide.

Printed in Great Britain
by Amazon